Chinese And American

A selective collection of Chinese dishes that combine well with any type of cooking—for luncheons, dinners, buffets, picnics, and barbecues.

This book will be treasured by people who enjoy Chinese food, for it demonstrates how beautifully one or two dishes can fit into a basically American meal.

For my grandmother, Harriet O. Hamilton

Without the help of Raeford Liles, the artist, this book would never have been written. His imaginative ideas and his practical aid in coordinating and testing recipes made it possible.

CHINESE COOKING WITH AMERICAN MEALS

MOIRA HODGSON

MODERN PROMOTIONS/PUBLISHERS
A Division of Unisystems, Inc. New York, New York 10022

Printed in Canada

Contents

Items followed by an asterisk
may be located by consulting the Index.

INTRODUCTION

Although interest in Chinese cooking has increased tremendously over the past few years, and Chinese restaurants have sprung up in almost every town, most people are still afraid to cook Chinese food at home. Only once in a while, for a special occasion, will the American cook collect all the necessary ingredients and make an effort to cook a complete meal served with chopsticks. But what she doesn't realize is that it is the simplest thing in the world to add a couple of Chinese dishes to a luncheon or dinner. A complete Chinese meal requires seven or eight dishes. This means juggling on the stove and careful timing. But individual dishes take no time at all to prepare and they are, in fact, quicker and easier to make than their American equivalents.

A thought which has occurred to few Americans before is that Chinese food mixes well with almost any type of cooking. You can use Chinese dishes with luncheons, dinners, buffets, for hors d'oeuvres, after-theater snacks, picnics, and barbecues. Many books have been written about Chinese cooking which require ingredients from Chinatown. But all the ingredients in this book are available at many supermarkets all over the country. The emphasis is not so much on using the authentic foodstuffs, but in finding good substitutes available to the American cook wherever in the country she may be.

You can make a Chinese dish in 15 minutes. It is certainly not complicated. Most dishes are cooked by frying the food very fast over a high flame in vegetable or peanut oil. Liquids are added and the food cooks for about 5 minutes. This way, the food retains the vitamins and minerals lost through long cooking. You can also prepare everything ahead of time by chopping up all the ingredients.

You'll find that Chinese food is very economical. Everything can be used again, be it rice, meat, or vegetables, and American leftovers can be recooked the Chinese way.

In this book we use American methods for cooking meat dishes, and give suggestions for Chinese dishes that will go with them. We also show ways of marinating meat, and give the recipes for some sauces and some complete simple Chinese dishes.

The purpose of this book is to make use of Chinese methods and ideas with American cooking. We are not trying to write a Chinese cookbook as such.

But if your friends and family are tired of the perennial "beef and two veg" dinners, the dreary salads produced at lunchtime, and the endless rounds of damp, soggy crackers served up at cocktail parties, here's a chance to get some variety into your meals in a way that's economical, dramatic, and quick.

INGREDIENTS

The following ingredients must always be in your kitchen:

Allspice

Anise seeds and powder

Bay leaves

Cornstarch

Curry powder

Flour (The Chinese use wheat flour.)

Garlic

Ginger (Use fresh when available but keep powdered ginger on hand.)

Mustard (Powdered Colman's is used in most recipes.)

Nutmeg

Oil (The Chinese use sesame oil, but this can be expensive. Use peanut or vegetable oil.)

Peppercorns (Black and white.)

Rosemary

Salt (Use rock salt which you grind yourself or kosher salt.)

Sherry (This is our substitute for rice wine and it must be dry. You can also use dry white wine, Japanese sake, or cognac.)

Soy Sauce (It comes in three different thicknesses. See page 22 for details.)

Sugar (Brown and white sugar are necessary.)

Tabasco sauce

Thyme

Turmeric

Vinegar

The following ingredients are not absolute essentials in your kitchen but it is a good idea to keep them on hand just in case:

Celery (Wash and store in refrigerator in plastic bag.)

Chicken stock (Make fresh and refrigerate. Boil once a week to kill germs. Stock will last six months this way.)

Chives (Buy frozen ones and substitute for scallion tops.)

Dried mushrooms (These are expensive but go a long way.)

Noodles (Large, flat kind.)

Onions

Parsley

Potatoes

Rice

Scallions (Wash, trim, and keep in refrigerator in plastic bag. Both the white and the green parts are used unless otherwise specified.)

Snow peas (Frozen.)

Spaghetti

Tomato purée or ketchup (The flavor of purée is better. Remove from can and keep in glass jar in refrigerator for a month.)

Vermicelli

Several Chinese sauces are available in bottled form and these are extremely useful. Keep them in the refrigerator.

Brown sauce

Chili sauce

Duk or plum sauce

Soy sauce

Sweet and sour sauce

Hoisin sauce

Oyster sauce

CHINESE FOODS AVAILABLE AT YOUR SUPERMARKET

We have been careful to use ingredients in this book that are available at supermarkets. Where this has not been possible we have chosen their closest substitutes. If you are looking for Chinese foods not available in the supermarket, and there are no Chinese stores in your town, we suggest you take a look in a health food store. Recipes for sauces used in this book are contained in chapter on sauces.

The following Chinese ingredients are available:

Anise powder or seeds
Bamboo shoots (canned)
Bean sprouts (canned)
Black beans (dry or canned)
Broth (canned chicken)

Brown sauce

Cinnamon

Chow mein (canned or frozen)

Dried mushrooms

Duk or plum sauce

Egg roll (frozen)

Noodles (see end of list)

Oyster sauce

Rice (see end of list)

Sesame oil

Snow peas (frozen)

Soy sauce (see end of list)

Tea (see end of list)

Water chestnuts (canned)

NOODLES

There are three main types of noodles available: rice noodles, wheat noodles, and thin Italian noodles (vermicelli). Although Chinese cellophane ones are available in some supermarkets, you may find that you'll have to use the Italian ones for the most part. If you can buy the Chinese ones, be very careful not to overcook them. Don't put them in the water until the diners are seated at the table. However, if you very much want to prepare them earlier you can cook them and drain them in a colander. When you are ready to use them pour boiling water over them.

Chinese and Italian methods for cooking noodles are the same. Cook an 8 ounce package for about 6 minutes in 2-3 quarts of boiling water. Drain them in a colander and run cold water over them to get rid of the starch.

There is an old restaurant trick for Italian noodles.

14

Cook them ahead of time until they are just soft outside and hard inside. Rinse in cold water and strain. Refrigerate. When you are ready to use them throw them into boiling water for 2 minutes. Lift out, drain, and serve. You'll have no starch and no coagulation.

If you wish to make a wonton soup you can substitute lasagna for the Chinese dumplings used.

RICE

Rice is the staple food of Southern China. In the North, however, wheat and grain are used. Different ways of cooking rice are given below; choose the method you prefer. The grains should be firm and separate, not soggy and stuck together.

1 cup rice to 1½ cups water

Wash the rice several times. Bring to boil, add salt, cover tightly and simmer for 20 minutes.

(You can use converted rice or Minute Rice as a substitute. Follow the directions on the package.)

To improve the flavor try some of the following suggestions:

Ginger
When you boil the rice put a couple of slices of ginger in the water.

Pre-fry
Fry the rice in 1 tablespoon peanut or vegetable oil. Pour in the water and cut down the cooking time by 5—10 minutes.

Broth
Instead of water use canned or fresh chicken broth. A bouillon cube may also be used but in that case use less salt.

Oyster Sauce*

Cook the rice in chicken broth and add 1 teaspoon oyster sauce to it.

Tea

Cook the rice in tea—having removed the leaves of course.

To keep the rice dry cover it with a cloth after it is cooked. This will absorb the steam.

Use more rice than you need and freeze the rest. You can use it later for Fried Rice*. It will keep about two months when frozen.

SOY SAUCE

There are many different brands and they vary in strength. Here are three good ones most commonly found in the supermarket.

China Beauty (thin and sweet)
La Choy (medium)
Kikkoman (Japanese, heavy and strong)

TEA

We will not go into the different brands of Chinese tea here, but you will find a wide variety at your supermarket. Tea is not, as most Americans think, drunk during the meal in China, but it is drunk after the meal. The tea is weak and delicate in flavor. Sugar and milk are never used.

Never soap out a teapot or you will ruin the flavor of the tea. Simply rinse it out with hot water. The water you use for making the tea should never be from the hot tap.

COOKING TECHNIQUES
AND PREPARATIONS

A Chinese cook prepares everything ahead of time. The ingredients are chopped to uniform size, parboiled or marinated if necessary, and placed on a plate or board ready for use. These preparations can be made in the morning and the food can be refrigerated in plastic bags. It will then be ready for cooking in the evening.

Always check to make sure that you have done the required amount of parboiling, soaking, and marinating before you start cooking. Once you begin you can't stop and the whole operation is over in about 15 minutes.

Don't start cooking until the guests are at the table. Chinese food cannot wait and must be served at once. It should always be put into heated dishes since it is not good served cold.

Timing is the secret to success. In most of the recipes we have tried to ensure that the cook will be able to keep the other food warm while she concentrates on the last-minute cooking of the Chinese dish (which, as we have said, takes only about 15 minutes).

CHOPPING

All ingredients used in Chinese-style cooking should be chopped to uniform size and shape so that they are easy to sauté. Americans can chop meat and vegetables a little larger than the Chinese do because they use forks instead of chopsticks.

Never wash your chopping block. Rub it down after use with a little bacon fat or vegetable oil.

When you slice let the knife do the work. Slice meats against the grain and when slicing irregularly shaped vegetables always start at the narrow end and work toward the thickest.

For slicing vegetables for salads, such as cucumber or carrots, use a potato peeler and you will get a very thin cut which will absorb the dressing easily. However don't add the dressing until you are just about to serve or the salad will be soggy.

The leaf, the stem, and the root of vegetables are cooked three different ways by the Chinese. They are also sliced differently since their cooking times are not the same. This is a different approach from the American style, in which the entire vegetable would be cooked the same way.

CUTTING TERMS

Chop Cut into very small pieces, uniform size
Cube Cut into 1-inch cubes
Dice Cut into ¼-inch cubes
Grate Rub on grater
Mince Cut very fine with knife or kitchen scissors

Shred   Cut into fine thread-like strips (can use potato peeler)

Slice   Cut into thin pieces

MEAT

Meat should be sliced against the grain. All fatty parts and bits of filament should be removed. It should be dried thoroughly on paper towels before it is cooked.

VEGETABLES

Firm vegetables should be sliced diagonally so that they cook more quickly. Tender vegetables should be sliced vertically.

Always add the tougher vegetables to the pan first.

Save celery leaves, cabbage leaves, for use in soups and stock.

COOKING

There are four methods of Chinese cooking used in this book: stewing, steaming, stir-frying, and deep-frying. Of these four the most often used and most difficult to master is the art of stir-frying. Once you can do this well you can consider yourself a Chinese cook.

Stir-frying

The ingredients are chopped. The skillet is heated, peanut or vegetable oil is added. When it is hot, add the garlic, ginger, and salt. Fry for about 30 seconds. Then add the ingredients and fry for about 2-3 minutes. In the case of vegetables the fibrous ones are added first, then the tender ones. If you are cooking chicken, add the dark meat first.

Timing is the key to stir-frying. If you think you are going too fast and the ingredients are burning, take the pan off the flame. Remember to toss the food constantly. Here two spoons would come in handy.

Serve the dish immediately. You must not start stir-frying until the diners are seated at the table. Otherwise the food will be soggy and unappetizing.

The hot oil seals in the juices of the meat and preserves its flavor. It also makes it more tender. This method is also excellent for vegetables since they retain their nutrients, their color, and their flavor. They have a crisp crunchy texture.

Deep-frying

The ingredients are chopped larger than the size used for stir-frying. They are often marinated in a soy sauce or sherry mixture, rolled in batter or cornstarch, and added piece by piece to hot deep fat. They are cooked until golden brown.

When the oil bubbles it is ready for fish, kidneys, or white meat. When it smokes it is ready for beef or pork.

The ingredients must be dry or they will spatter and become soggy. Add them little by little to the pan otherwise you will reduce the temperature of the oil. When they are done drain on paper towels.

If you have cooked fish in the oil you can remove the fishy taste by dropping in a potato, which will absorb it. You can then store the oil for future use. Another way to remove any traces of the frying is to refrigerate the oil. The impurities will rise to the surface and can be scraped off.

Stewing

Like Americans, the Chinese use this method for cooking meat. There are two different kinds of stewing: red stewing, which uses soy sauce and is used for lamb, pork, or beef, and white stewing, which uses fish and chicken stewed in a clear broth. A heavy Dutch oven is good for this method.

Steaming

This is a very good way to cook duck since it gets rid of the fat. A rack is set in a pan of boiling water and a Pyrex dish is set on the rack. The water should come about two-thirds up the side of the dish.

KITCHEN EQUIPMENT AND UTENSILS

Every dish in this book can be prepared and cooked with the equipment found in a normal American kitchen. There are however certain items that are especially useful for Chinese-style cooking. You would be wise to check the equipment listed here against that of your own kitchen and invest in that which you do not have. You won't find it expensive.

POTS AND PANS

A *wok*. This is used by the Chinese for stir-frying foods. You can buy one easily if you live in New York or San Francisco but for those who are unable to obtain one there are many excellent substitutes. To keep the wok clean, rinse immediately with cold water and wipe dry with paper towels.

American substitutes for a wok:

A large *frying pan*, heavy-bottomed, with a lid.

A large *omelet pan* with scooped sides. The food can be tossed without fear of spilling. The pan must be large enough since a pan that is too small will overcrowd ingredients. Thus some will burn and some will not cook and you'll have no room to toss.

A large *Teflon frying pan*. Use a wooden spoon or plastic spatula to avoid scraping off the no-stick treatment. This is a good pan since it does not burn the food.

A *deep electric skillet*. This is good in that it ensures even heat. It should have a rounded bottom to facilitate tossing. The skillet can also be put on the table and comes in most useful for parties and buffets.

A *deep frying pan with a basket*. This is essential for deep-fried foods. After you've deep-fried fish or shrimp in it drop a potato in the oil. It will take the fish taste out of it so that it can be used again.

A *heavy pot for stewing*. You can use a large heavy pot that goes on top of the stove, but you would be better off with a large casserole that can be used either for cooking on top of the stove or for baking in the oven. You can also bring these attractive casseroles to the table and serve from them.

Useful are pans that can be put on the top of the stove, in the oven, used for storing food in the refrigerator or freezer and for serving at the table. You can buy these dishes in all sizes.

A *tall deep pot* for rice. This is essential to stop the rice from boiling over.

A *double boiler* for keeping foods warm or reheating leftovers.

Knife with wide blade, 6 inches long.

Knife with serrated edge.

Small paring knife.

Teaspoons and tablespoons for measuring.

Two large metal or wooden spoons for tossing foods.

Spatula with holes in it for fried foods. Use a plastic one with a Teflon frying pan.

If you are using the same spoon or knife for different foods, keep a bowl of hot water nearby. You can dip it in to rinse and you won't get the flavors mixed up.

Garlic press. To make it easier to clean put in a small piece of cheesecloth. Then add the garlic and squeeze through. Lift out the cheesecloth and you will find that all those awkward little pieces will come out with it.

Potato peeler.

Grater with holes of all sizes.

Onion chopper. This is a great help in Chinese cooking where so much chopping and shredding is required.

Three mixing bowls from 2-quart to 2-cup size.

Plastic bowls for freezing sauces.

Small Chinese bowls for serving and storing sauces in the refrigerator.

Good thick chopping block, about 8 by 8 inches for meat. To clean it wipe it down with oil. Never soap it. It is a good idea to keep another chopping block for vegetables.

Blender for sauces, etc.

Salad tosser. This is useful for drying vegetables before they are stir-fried, and does not take as long as the paper towel method.

Small wooden pepper grinder for kitchen use.

OTHER KITCHEN EQUIPMENT

Aluminum foil. This is essential for storing or reheating foods. You can also reheat different foods in the same dish by using foil as a divider.

Kitchen paper towels. You'll need these for draining fried foods and drying washed vegetables and meat before they are fried.

Plastic bags. Use for keeping chopped foods. Chop ahead of time and store in refrigerator. You can do the same with parboiled vegetables. Then everything is ready when you are about to cook. Also use them for tossing foods in cornstarch or flour. Pour the flour into the bag and toss the food around in it. It's much less messy than rolling food on a floured board or plate.

Cheesecloth. Useful for herb bouquets, spreading over rice to absorb moisture, and cleaning garlic press.

Glass jars of all different sizes. These are great for storing foods, sauces, etc. Use candy, coffee, or little baby food jars and keep in an easy accessible place. Mark dates on the jars so you'll know how old the contents are.

Stove. Gas burners are the most effective for Chinese cooking since they give an intense concentration of heat and turn off quickly. If using electric heat, and you wish to turn it down during stir-frying, lift the pan off the stove. The food will keep on cooking but will not burn.

SERVING AND DECORATION

TABLE DECORATION

There are countless ways in which you can add a Chinese touch to your table. Chinese dishes are very inexpensive and easily obtainable.

Buy bowls in different colors so that if they break you don't have to replace the same pattern. The bright colors are cheerful and decorative, and the bowls are ideal for rice, soup, or dips.

Use small Chinese side dishes for mustards and cold sauces as dips.

Serve bowls on top of cups to make a Chinese serving dish.

Buy some individual earthenware Chinese soup spoons. They're great for soups and sauces.

Buy some Chinese teacups.

Put out brightly colored woven table mats.

Once in a while buy some short fat candles.

Make a centerpiece with lilies, poppies, or chrysanthemums. Don't make it so large that you can't see the guest across it.

SERVING

When you serve soup you can put a large tureen on the table and let everyone help himself. Good soup pots are the ones that have removable handles and can be taken from the stove to the table.

For the soup use a large ladle.

Your guests can make their own soup in a Chinese way. In little bowls put chopped shrimp, endive, avocado, onion, meat, and egg shreds (egg cooked like an omelet and cut into shreds). Let the guests help themselves to these and pour the hot soup over them.

Always heat your plates in the oven before serving but don't bake them. Another good way of heating them is to run them under a very hot water tap and wipe them off.

A chafing dish on the table is a very good way of keeping food warm.

Use an airtight lid over the rice to keep it hot. If you can find a bamboo steamer it would be excellent for this purpose.

Keep the food covered at all times.

Buy a good large serving dish with sloping sides to serve meat dishes over rice.

Place individual dishes of soy sauce, Chinese mustard, etc., on the table. Allow one dish between two people.

Buy some small wooden salt shakers and pepper grinders for the table.

Keep sauces hot in a chafing dish.

Let color be your guide when serving Chinese food. Be liberal with fresh parsley, chopped tomatoes, red or green peppers, chopped scallions, shredded egg, shredded leftover meat for effect. The look of the food is extremely important.

HELPFUL HINTS

SEASONING AND FLAVORING

Always use rock or kosher salt, fresh ground pepper.

Always taste vinegar before you use it. A new bottle may be of a different strength.

Ac'cent may be used in Chinese cooking. See note in "On Reading the Recipes." When you use canned broth, omit Ac'cent.

A drop of sesame oil in a bottle of peanut oil will give it the real Chinese flavor—and save money.

Always keep a bottle of dry sherry in your kitchen. Domestic sherry is not expensive and makes all the difference to your cooking.

Never use sweet sherry or sweet wine in Chinese cooking.

To make a Chinese ginger-sherry slice some fresh ginger (if available) and put it into a pint of sherry. Leave it for a week and you'll have a perfect ginger sherry.

If fresh ginger is unavailable you can achieve a

similar effect by adding 2 teaspoons of powdered ginger to the sherry and leaving it for a week.

Simmer chicken bones in water to make stock.

Always save chicken giblets, feet, and bones for stock.

Don't use beef stock or broth; it is usually too strong for the delicate flavor of Chinese food.

To remove fat from stock cool stock in refrigerator and remove fat in one piece.

Bouillon cubes tend to be salty, so cut down seasoning if used.

Keep cooking fats in different containers, according to flavor, in the refrigerator for future use.

Save vegetable water for soups and stocks.

Save water from canned vegetables (except Chinese vegetables) for soups and stocks.

Save leafy tops of vegetables for soups and stocks.

Save the fat that you lift off soups and stocks and use it for cooking later.

Never cook anything in plain water, always use stock.

Purée of baby foods strengthens the flavor of sauces and fillings.

Buy a thicker soy sauce and water down for table use—economize.

A pinch of curry powder often improves a dish that "lacks something."

Freeze celery leaves (like chives), chop them up, and scatter them over food for flavor and decoration.

When stuffing turkey buy an extra packet of chicken gizzards and giblets for added flavor.

Buy a spice shelf so that your spices are always easily within reach.

Keep jars of oyster sauce, ginger wine, and hot pepper sauce ready in the refrigerator.

To cure fresh pineapple for use in Chinese pineapple dishes, skin, core, and remove hard bits. Spread sugar and water over the slices and let stand to soften.

To get a charcoal-broiled flavor on chops, sprinkle them with charcoal powder and lemon juice, wrap in foil paper, and bake in oven, opening paper for last 10 minutes to get broiled coat.

Don't add extra sugar if a Sweet and Sour sauce is too bitter. A little grated carrot will do the trick, but extra sugar does not cancel out the vinegar.

Never mix in cornstarch unless you've mixed it with a little liquid first.

Baby foods are excellent in sauces if you don't have a blender.

Add a teaspoonful of baby food to omelet fillings for added flavor.

Try a squeeze of lemon or a dash of soy sauce to make a dish tastier.

Use scallion tops to scatter over food as the Italians use parsley, or the French use chives.

Add salad dressings just before you serve the salad unless otherwise specified.

Decorate dishes with paprika.

The day before a party, remove ice from trays and store in plastic bags in freezer. Refill and empty ice cube trays several times. This way you will have enough ice for the party.

Give a new flavor to salad dressing by adding soy sauce to taste.

To make bread crumbs, grind leftover bread in the blender, season with herbs, place in an airtight container and refrigerate. They will keep for several weeks.

COOKING

Never put food in cold oil when you are cooking. It will come out greasy and soggy.

Heat skillet before you add oil.

When cooking vegetables in oil keep stirring. A Teflon pan would come in handy here, so that the food would not stick.

To test oil temperature, drop in a piece of bread. If it sizzles, the fat is ready.

To keep food warm at lowest possible temperature use asbestos pad between pan and heat source.

Ingredients should be added to the pan a few at a time to keep the temperature of the oil from going down.

Always dry food before you fry it.

Braised dishes can be prepared in extra portions which you can serve at subsequent meals. They need only be reheated and refried. This is usually done in restaurants.

When the oil begins to sizzle add salt, then the vegetables. It makes them a brighter green.

Vegetables especially must be absolutely dry before they are fried. Either dry them on paper towels or shake them in a salad twirler.

Food keeps on cooking even after it is taken off the flame. Don't wait until it's absolutely ready or you may overcook it.

Chinese food should always be underdone rather than overdone.

Never overcook Chinese rice. The grains should be separate. If you do overcook, say you're doing it Japanese style.

When deep-frying in hot peanut oil, put in a lettuce leaf at the end. It will absorb the fat.

When you parboil vegetables rinse them immediately in cold water to prevent their cooking further. If you leave them hot, they continue to cook. That is why rice and vegetables are so often overdone.

Use a large frying pan rather than a small one. You can toss the food without spilling and the food will cook evenly.

When ingredients are tough, cutting them into small chunks makes them more absorbent and less tough.

Noodles should never be added cold to hot soup. They should be reheated or added hot.

Don't use a pressure cooker for any Chinese recipes. It overcooks the food.

Always rinse spaghetti and noodles in cold water to stop them from cooking and to wash off the starch.

To peel tomatoes and almonds drop them into boiling water for a minute and slip off their skins.

When using a portion of a package of frozen food saw off the amount you need without thawing the entire contents.

Never let food get cold slowly; refrigerate it immediately. This prevents spoilage and possible food poisoning.

THE CHINESE WAY

Ingredients are never cooked alone, as in Western-style cooking.

Seasoning is always done in the kitchen, not at the table.

Sauces are always served at the table.

Chinese foods can be prepared the day before. For example you can cook a whole chicken, cut it up, and cook it the Chinese way the next day.

Chop your ingredients the day before and keep them fresh in a plastic bag.

Always buy a little more meat than you need and save the leftovers for use in a Chinese meal later.

Fried rice can be frozen and reheated in the same dish that it was frozen in.

You can often add shredded leftover meat or chopped scallions for decoration.

If you are in a hurry and don't have any leftover meat you can buy slices of salami, pressed ham, etc. and slice into matchsticks. This can be used for decoration or as a meal, served over noodles.

To improve beans soaked overnight, add soy sauce,

Ac'cent, ginger, and a chopped onion to the liquid.

Use biscuit dough as a substitute for dumpling mixture.

Use a teaspoon of red coloring for basting roasts—this is a Chinese trick and adds color to the gravy.

Fresh Jerusalem artichokes make an excellent substitute for canned water chestnuts.

Never throw a bone away. You can always use them in soups and stocks.

To improve a Chinese stuffed avocado, scoop out a larger area of avocado and mix it in with the stuffing.

If you cannot buy scallions, use small seed onions or garlic salt.

Remember texture is as important as taste so don't mix chopped foods with grated unless you have a reason.

Store half cans of bamboo shoots, water chestnuts, etc., in baby food jars in the refrigerator. Plan leftovers to go with them.

To chop parsley and cube soft meats use kitchen scissors. Chop parsley in a cup.

When preparing Chinese foods, let color and texture be your guide.

For an attractive presentation, serve fried rice in baked green peppers.

A quick lunch with a Chinese tone: Crush a garlic clove, chop parsley, and mix with oil and seasonings. Serve over thin delicate Chinese noodles.

Use green spinach noodles in place of Chinese noodles.

SHOPPING

Save money by buying unripe avocados and letting them ripen for a week. If you refrigerate them the ripening process will stop.

Buy boned chicken breasts. You lose a lot of meat by doing it yourself.

Save money by buying house brands of canned goods.

When buying ground meat, get the butcher to cut up the portion in front of you so that you know what you are buying.

ON READING THE RECIPES

We have not specified, except in certain cases, the amount of salt and pepper to use. This should be determined by taste. You can never lay down the rules for seasoning. The only way to achieve the correct result is by experiment.

The Chinese use a salt of vegetable protein (monosodium glutamate) which heightens the flavor of food. It can be bought here most commonly under the name of Ac'cent. While it can improve the flavor of dish it can also wipe out its subtle distinction if used too liberally. Recent investigations have also suggested that it may be dangerous if used too much. Thus we have not indicated Ac'cent in the recipes, but leave its use to the discretion of the cook.

Chinese dried mushrooms are the kind used in most of the recipes unless otherwise specified. These should be soaked in water, preferably overnight, or for at least half an hour before they are used. Save the water for flavoring soups and gravies. Fresh mushrooms may be substituted but they do not have the same taste at all.

Fresh ginger is available in some supermarkets, but if you are unable to obtain it leave it out. In some cases we specify the use of powdered ginger as a substitute because it adds an interesting flavor to certain dishes. However it does not have the same taste as fresh ginger.

When a recipe calls for scallions, use the entire scallion including the green part unless otherwise specified.

We have not specified cooking times for these recipes because in most cases the cooking will take 15 minutes. The chopping and cutting take longer and the length of time this takes depends upon how adept the cook is.

Since many of the recipes require marinating, overnight soaking, and parboiling, you would be wise to read them right through before you start cooking.

In the menus, the names of Chinese dishes appear in large capital letters, those of American dishes in small capital letters.

SAUCES

The Chinese sauces listed here are called for in recipes throughout the book. They are simple to make and keep for several weeks in the refrigerator. They make an interesting addition to any meal and add flavor to even an entirely American dinner.

CANTONESE LOBSTER SAUCE

1 clove garlic
3 scallions
¼ lb. minced pork
1 tblsp. dry sherry
1 tblsp. soy sauce
½ tsp. sugar
3 tblsp. peanut or vegetable oil

1 tsp. cornstarch mixed with
1 tsp. water
2 beaten eggs
Salt and pepper

Mince the garlic and chop the scallions. To pork add sherry, soy sauce, sugar. Heat oil in skillet. Quick-fry garlic and scallions. Add pork mixture to

39

pan. Cook for 10 minutes until pork is thoroughly done (it should be white.) Add cornstarch mixture; when sauce thickens to coat the spoon add beaten eggs. Season and serve at once. Makes about 1½ cups.

Note: *This sauce is particularly good with shellfish.*

OYSTER SAUCE

1 can (3¾ oz.) smoked oysters	1 bouillon cube (chicken)
½ c. sherry	2 tblsp. soy sauce
½ c. water	Salt and pepper
	Dash sugar

Mince oysters and bring to boil with their liquid in sherry, water, bouillon cube, soy sauce, seasoning, and sugar. Simmer for 20 minutes. Strain into jar and refrigerate. Makes about 1½ cups.

Note: *Saved mince oysters for addition to leftover meal.*

DUK (PLUM) SAUCE

½ c. chutney	1 tblsp. sugar
1 c. plum jelly	1 tsp. vinegar

Chop chutney and mix with plum jelly. Heat sugar and vinegar over low heat. Mix all ingredients together and refrigerate until ready for use. Makes about 1½ cups.

Note: *You can add baby food apricot purée, or applesauce to this for extra flavor.*

BLACK BEAN SAUCE

½ c. drained mashed black beans (either canned or soaked overnight)
2 tblsp. peanut or vegetable oil
1 clove garlic, crushed

1 tblsp. cornstarch mixed with
1 tblsp. water
½ c. water
3 scallions, chopped
Salt and pepper

Mash drained black beans. Heat oil in skillet and stir-fry garlic. Add beans and cornstarch mixture and water. Cook until thick (about 2 minutes). Add chopped scallions to sauce. Season and serve. Makes 1½ cups.

SZECHWAN SAUCE

2 chili peppers
2 slices fresh ginger
1 clove garlic
3 tblsp. Tabasco sauce
½ c. dry sherry

⅓ c. soy sauce
1 tsp. sugar
Salt and pepper
2 tblsp. peanut or vegetable oil

Mince peppers, ginger, and garlic finely. Mix together Tabasco, sherry, soy sauce, sugar, and seasoning. In skillet heat oil. Quick-fry peppers, ginger, and garlic, for about 2 minutes. Add Tabasco-soy mixture and bring to boil. Remove from heat and serve at once. Makes about 1 cup.

Note: *This sauce is particularly good with shellfish.*

MANDARIN SAUCE

1 tblsp. peanut or vegetable oil
2 scallions, chopped
2 cloves garlic, crushed
2 slices ginger, chopped
4 Chinese dried mushrooms, soaked in water overnight (or for 30 min.)

½ c. soy sauce
2 tblsp. dry sherry
1 tblsp. brown sugar
Salt and pepper
1 c. chicken stock
1 tsp. cornstarch mixed with
1 tsp. water

Heat oil in skillet. Add scallions, garlic, and ginger and stir-fry for 2 minutes. Drain mushrooms, chop, and add to pan; stir-fry 1 minute. Add soy sauce, sherry, sugar, and seasoning. Add chicken stock and bring to boil. Add cornstarch mixture and boil until sauce is thick enough to coat spoon. Makes about 1½ cups.

Note: *This sauce is excellent with fish.*

BEAN SPROUT SAUCE

1 can (8 oz.) black beans, drained (or 1 c. dried, soaked in water overnight and drained)
½ c. peanut or vegetable oil
1 clove garlic, crushed
2 small onions, grated
½ tsp. salt

Juice ½ lemon
1 can (5 oz.) bean sprouts, drained
2 tblsp. dry sherry
1 tsp. soy sauce
1 tsp. cornstarch mixed with
1 tsp. water
Salt and pepper

Mash black beans. Heat oil in skillet. Add garlic, onions, and salt. Fry for 1 minute and add beans. Add lemon juice. Add drained bean sprouts; stir and cook for 2 minutes. Add sherry, soy sauce, cornstarch mixture, and seasoning. Stir until sauce thickens enough to coat spoon. Makes 2 cups.

BROWN SAUCE

½ can (5 oz.) bamboo shoots, drained
2 chili peppers
4 Chinese dried mushrooms, soaked in water overnight (or for 30 min.)

2 tblsp. peanut or vegetable oil
4 tblsp. bottled chiang (Chinese brown sauce)
Salt and pepper

Chop bamboo shoots, peppers, and drained mushrooms. In skillet heat oil. Stir-fry vegetables for 2 minutes. Add *chiang* and season. Cook for 2 more minutes and serve. Makes 1½ cups.

HOT MUSTARD

1-2 c. water	½ c. powdered mustard

Add water gradually to mustard so that it turns into a smooth paste.

Serve as a dip in small dishes, or add as a flavoring to recipes requiring Chinese mustard.

Note: *You can improve the flavor of the mustard by adding beer instead of water. You can also add 1 teaspoon soy sauce to the mustard.*

SESAME PASTE

4 tblsp. water	1 tsp. sesame seeds
4 tblsp. peanut butter	Salt and pepper
1 tblsp. sesame or peanut oil	

Mix all ingredients together to form a smooth paste. Serve the mixture in a dip dish. Makes about 1 cup.

SWEET AND SOUR SAUCE

¾ c. water	1 tblsp. soy sauce
½ c. brown sugar	Pinch salt
½ c. vinegar	
1 tsp. cornstarch mixed with	
1 tblsp. water	

Bring water to boil. Add sugar, cook for 1 minute, and add vinegar. Turn down heat and cook until sugar has melted. Add cornstarch mixture, soy sauce,

43

and salt. Stir so sauce thickens and coats spoon. Makes about 2 cups.

Note: *If the sauce is too sour, don't add more sugar, add grated carrot. You can also add a touch of red food coloring or tomato paste.*

VEGETABLES

The Chinese were the first to discover the nutritional value of raw or partially cooked vegetables. Since millions of Chinese were Buddhists and therefore vegetarians, they perfected the form of cooking which has become the most outstanding method today. Raw vegetables were not eaten since they could be dangerous. But they discovered a way of cooking vegetables so lightly that the germs were destroyed while the vitamins and minerals were maintained. We show here the Chinese way of cooking vegetables and give some hints on buying and cooking.

Buying

Avoid tough, overgrown vegetables.

The largest does not mean the best quality. Look for smaller vegetables. They will be younger, tenderer, and more flavorful. The extra work in peeling and cleaning is worth it.

Buy too little rather than too much. Vegetables do not keep well.

Don't be duped by tired old vegetables on sale.

When you are buying leafy vegetables make sure they look firm and crisp.

Cooking

Don't overcook vegetables so that they become soft and mushy. They should have a bright green, not an olive color.

Avoid frozen vegetables if possible when you are cooking the Chinese way. They turn out less crisp and have less flavor. If you cannot avoid using them, thaw and dry them completely first. Then fry them briefly in oil.

When cooking different vegetables together, add those needing longer cooking time first and the tender ones last.

When cooking leafy vegetables add the stalks first and the leaves last.

Never add more liquid than absolutely necessary when stir-frying or the vegetable will lose its crispness.

Cook in chicken, not beef, stock. The latter is too strong.

Be careful when adding soy sauce to vegetables. If you add too much you will destroy the subtle taste.

When you add liquid to the pan, pour it down the sides, not directly onto the vegetables. It will heat faster and the vegetables will keep their crispness.

Vegetables that are not leafy can be cooked in advance and reheated by being stir-fried quickly in oil.

Stir-frying: This is the best method of cooking vegetables. They are quickly stir-fried in hot oil, which seals in their juices and brings out their flavor. A little stock or soy sauce is added at the end and the vegetable, depending upon its texture, is cooked for a few more minutes. The vitamin content of the vegetable is kept since there are no excess liquids to pour down the drain.

To make a sweet and sour vegetable add a teaspoon of sugar and a tablespoon of vinegar at the end.

When you have prepared the vegetable according to the chart below, heat the frying pan. Add a small amount of peanut oil and when it begins to sizzle add salt (rock salt is the best). This will make the vegetable a brighter green. Then add the vegetable. The juices will soon be rendered up and it will cook in them. Keep stirring so that it does not stick to the pan. Then add the liquid after about 2 or 3 minutes according to the chart. Never use more liquid than absolutely necessary. Cover the pan and steam until the vegetable is done.

Vegetable Chart

The chart is divided into three parts. In the first section you will find vegetables that must be parboiled (dropped for 2 minutes into boiling water) before they are cooked. They are then stir-fried, covered (unless directed otherwise), and cooked for a few minutes in liquid.

The second group of vegetables is soft. They should be peeled, sliced, stir-fried, and cooked for a few minutes in liquid.

The third group requires no parboiling at all and some of the vegetables here need no additional liquid.

I

	Preparation	Cooking
Asparagus	Cut up diagonally, 1½ inches long. Parboil except tips. Drain and dry.	Stir-fry. Add stalks first. Cook 2-3 minutes in liquid.

	Preparation	*Cooking*
Broccoli	Cut into flowerets. Parboil.	Stir-fry. Cook 5 minutes in liquid, covered, 1 minute uncovered.
Brussels Sprouts	Cut in half if large. Parboil.	Stir-fry. Cook 2-3 minutes in liquid.
Carrots	Chop diagonally. Parboil.	Stir-fry. Cook 3 minutes in liquid.
Cauliflower	Break into flowerets. Parboil.	Stir-fry. Cook 3 minutes in liquid.
Potatoes	Peel and cut into slices. Parboil.	Stir-fry. Cook 3-5 minutes in liquid.
String Beans	Chop diagonally into 1½-inch slices. Parboil.	Stir-fry. Cook 4-5 minutes in liquid.
Turnips	Cut into slices. Parboil.	Stir-fry. Cook 4-5 minutes in liquid.

II

	Preparation	*Cooking*
Cucumber	Peel. Slice thinly.	Stir-fry. Cook 3-4 minutes in liquid.
Eggplant	Peel, slice into chunks. Let stand salted for 15 minutes.	Stir-fry. Cook 13 minutes in liquid.
Squash	Peel, slice.	Stir-fry. Cook 3-4 minutes in liquid.
Zucchini	Peel, slice.	Stir-fry. Cook 4-5 minutes in liquid (if not peeled, cook 6 minutes in liquid).

	Preparation	Cooking
Bamboo Shoots (canned)	Drain and slice thinly. Dry.	Stir-fry. Cook 2-3 minutes in liquid.
Bean Sprouts (canned)	Drain and dry.	Stir-fry. Cook 2-3 minutes in liquid.
Cabbage	Shred coarsely.	Stir-fry. No additional liquid required. Cook covered for 2-3 minutes.
Celery	Cut in 1½-inch pieces.	Stir-fry. Cook for 2 minutes in liquid.
Green Pepper	Same as above.	Stir-fry. Cook for 2 minutes in liquid— keep crisp.
Lettuce	Shred.	Stir-fry. No additional liquid required. Cook covered for 2-3 minutes.
Mushrooms (fresh)	Wash and dry.	Stir-fry. Cook for 2-3 minutes, covered. No additional liquid required.
Mushrooms (dried)	Soak in water for 30 minutes or overnight. Drain and dry.	Stir-fry. Cook 3-5 minutes in soaking liquid.
Mustard Cabbage	Slice coarsely. Separate stalks.	Stir-fry. Cook 2-3 minutes in liquid. Cook stalks 1 minute longer, adding them first.
Onions	Slice and chop.	Stir-fry. Cook for 2 minutes in liquid.
Peas	Remove pod.	Stir-fry. Cook for 3-4 minutes in liquid.

	Preparation	*Cooking*
Snow Peas (frozen)	Thaw and dry.	Stir-fry. No additional liquid required. Do not cover.
Spinach	Wash, cut in 1½-inch lengths.	Stir-fry. No additional liquid. Cover and cook 2-3 minutes.
Swiss Chard	Shred coarsely.	Stir-fry. Cook for 4 minutes in liquid.
Tomatoes	Slice or cut in segments.	Stir-fry. No additional liquid required.
Water Chestnuts (canned)	Drain, slice diagonally and dry.	Stir-fry. Cook 2-3 minutes in liquid (do not cover).

HORS D'OEUVRES

In China there exist restaurants that serve only tea and hors d'oeuvres. These are equivalent to the coffeehouses of the West—only without the sweet desserts and cakes that are normally found in the latter.

Chinese hors d'oeuvres are light and appetizing without filling you up before a meal, or giving you indigestion (as pretzels and potato chips are apt to do). They should be served very hot if they are cooked and are usually accompanied by dips in small Chinese dishes.

If they are hot, we suggest you serve them in a chafing dish. Cold ones should be served on a large dish with the dip in the middle so that guests can help themselves to both when they are handed around. Decorate the plate with parsley or scallions or baby tomatoes sliced in half for color.

BARBECUED SPARERIBS

The Chinese were barbecuing 5,000 years ago, before Texas was even thought of. And in many households they still cook their food over charcoal. But they add an extra touch which makes their meat taste quite different from anything you would find on a Texas ranch. They marinate it in soy sauce overnight, then they proceed just as the Texans would. You can do these ribs outside over the charcoal, or in the oven. If you are cooking outside, you can cut down on your cooking time by baking the meat first in the oven and simply reheating it over the coals.

3 ribs per person

Marinade (for 12 ribs)

Don't be afraid to use your imagination. The ingredients listed here, with the exception of the soy sauce, oil, and seasonings, are easily replaced by something else, or left out altogether, depending on what you're mixing with the ribs. If you're serving many sweet things, perhaps you'd rather cut out the honey and the sugar.

2 tsp. peanut or vegetable oil
1 garlic clove, crushed
1 tblsp. soy sauce
¼ c. chicken stock
3 chili peppers, chopped (optional)
1 tsp. chili sauce (optional)
2 tblsp. honey (optional)
2 tblsp. sugar (optional)
2 tblsp. dry sherry (optional)
Salt and pepper

Mix all ingredients together in a large dish (not a metal dish) and place the ribs so that they are completely covered by the mixture. Soak at least 6 hours. Preheat oven to 375° F. Roast about 15 minutes on each side, until brown, basting with the marinade mixture.

Duk Sauce* would go well. You can buy this bottled or make it yourself with plum jelly and chutney. Also you could try Oyster Sauce* or Sweet and Sour Sauce*.

EGG ROLL

This can be a difficult recipe to make until you are adept at handling the egg sheets in which the mixture is wrapped. If you fry them too thin they will crumble and fall apart.

You can buy frozen egg rolls in the supermarket. Heat them up and serve them with hot Sweet and Sour Sauce*, either bottled or according to the recipe listed in the Index.

½ lb. ground pork
2 tsp. dry sherry
2 tsp. soy sauce
1 tsp. grated ginger
1 tsp. grated orange peel
    (optional)
2 tblsp. canned soy beans
2 tblsp. chopped onion
2 tsp. cornstarch mixed
    with
2 tsp. water

Salt and pepper
4 eggs
1 tblsp. peanut or vegetable oil
3 tblsp. flour
3 tblsp. water
4 c. peanut or vegetable oil
Paprika (optional)
Sweet and Sour Sauce*

In a bowl mix together pork, sherry, soy sauce, ginger, orange peel, soy beans, onions, and cornstarch mixture. Season and divide mixture into 8 portions. Beat eggs, season and in large skillet fry in oil. Cut into 8 thin squares. Place portion of mixture in each square. Mix flour with water and use as a paste to seal squares over mixture. In skillet heat oil. Deep-fry egg rolls until golden. Drain and place on heated dish. Cut three incisions across the rolls. If desired scatter a little paprika over them for decoration. Serve with the Sweet and Sour Sauce* in a separate dish. Serves 8.

COCKTAIL BALLS

Serve these in a chafing dish with toothpicks. You can use minced leftover chicken or meat in place of the crab meat. Sprinkle the balls with a little chopped parsley for decoration when you serve them.

1 can (7 oz.) crab meat	1 tblsp. water
½ onion	Salt and pepper
1 tsp. soy sauce	2 c. peanut or vegetable
1 egg	oil
¼ c. cooked rice	
1 tblsp. cornstarch mixed with	

Mince crab meat and onion. Place in bowl and add soy sauce. Beat egg. Add to bowl. Add rice, cornstarch mixture, and seasoning. Mix together and form into balls golf ball size. Heat oil in skillet. Deep-fry the balls until golden brown. Drain and serve in chafing dish. Makes about 24.

STUFFED EGGS WITH BEAN SPROUTS

After you have hard-boiled the eggs, take out one yolk and set it aside. This way if you find that the stuffing is too runny you can thicken it by adding the yolk.

6 hard-boiled eggs	½ tsp. Tabasco sauce
1 can (7 oz.) bean sprouts, drained	½ tsp. curry powder
1 tblsp. soy sauce	Salt and pepper
1 tsp. peanut or vegetable oil	Paprika

Halve eggs and remove yolks. Chop bean sprouts very fine and mash in with the egg yolks. Add soy sauce, oil, Tabasco, curry powder, and seasoning. Turn the mixture into the egg halves. For decoration sprinkle with paprika and serve. Makes 12.

CHINESE DEVILED EGGS

For a change from the usual stuffed or deviled eggs that you find at most cocktail parties, stuff the eggs with something a little different. This filling is very economical and it looks good too.

6 hard-boiled eggs	2 tsp. sesame oil (or vegetable or peanut oil)
2 scallions	
1 can (7 oz.) crab meat, drained	1 tsp. lemon juice
1 tsp. dry mustard	Salt and pepper
½ c. soy sauce	¼ tsp. paprika

Chop scallions very fine. Mix together crab meat, mustard, soy sauce, oil, lemon juice, and seasoning. Slice eggs in half. Remove hardened yolk. Mix in with crab meat stuffing. Stuff halved eggs with mixture. For effect sprinkle with paprika. Makes 12 stuffed eggs.

EGG AND WATERCRESS DIP FOR CELERY

Everyone is tired of the usual dips that go with celery. But here's a recipe for a sauce that is different and a little spicy.

6 hard-boiled eggs	1 tsp. soy sauce
1 bunch watercress	1 tsp. dry mustard
2 tblsp. peanut or vegetable oil	Salt and pepper
	2 bunches celery
3 tsp. white wine vinegar	3 scallion tops

Chop eggs finely. Wash watercress. Keep it tied for the first wash. Cut off the stems. Untie and wash again. Chop finely. In a bowl mix oil, vinegar, soy sauce, mustard, and seasoning. Add eggs and watercress and mix. Wash the celery. Either use the sauce as a dip for the celery stalks or stuff the stalks with it.

Chop the scallion tops and sprinkle over mixture, whether in a bowl or over the stuffed stalks. Serves 6-8.

CHICKEN WINGS

These can be cooked in the morning and reheated in oil and seasonings just before you need them. Serve them hot, preferably in a chafing dish. Use Oyster Sauce* and soy sauce as dips.

15	chicken wings	4	tsp. peanut or vegetable oil
2	c. chicken stock	¼	c. Oyster Sauce*
1	onion, roughly chopped	3	tblsp. soy sauce
1	stalk celery	1	tblsp. sugar
1	bay leaf	1	tsp. vinegar
1	clove garlic	4	ginger slices, chopped
1	tsp. salt		Salt and pepper

Cut off the wing tips and hold for future use in stock. Wash and dry the wings. Bring to boil stock, onion, celery, bay leaf, garlic, salt, and 1 teaspoon oil. Add wings and cook for 5-7 minutes. Drain and dry, reserving one-quarter of the stock. To remainder add Oyster Sauce*, soy sauce, sugar, and vinegar. Bring to boil, add wings, and cook for 20 minutes until tender. Drain and dry. Wrap in plastic bag until ready for use. Heat remaining oil, ginger slices, and seasoning in skillet. Turn chicken wings quickly in the mixture to brown and reheat. Serve at once. Serves 6-8.

CHICKEN LIVER AND ALMOND CANAPES

These little sandwiches can be served hot or cold and sprinkled with chopped parsley for decoration.

1 lb. chicken livers	1 tblsp. soy sauce
8 scallions	Salt and pepper
3 tblsp. peanut or vegetable oil	Whole wheat bread, crusts removed
1/4 lb. sliced, blanched almonds	Chopped parsley (optional)

Remove white filament from livers and slice in half. Chop scallions finely. In skillet heat oil. Sauté scallions for 1 minute. Add almonds. Sauté 1 minute. Add livers and stir-fry for about 4 minutes. Add soy sauce, cook another minute, season, and remove from pan. In a bowl mash the chicken liver mixture with a fork. Spread it thinly over whole wheat bread and make into open sandwiches 2 inches square. Makes about 24.

CHICKEN LIVERS WITH BACON AND WATER CHESTNUTS

To make sure that the bacon does not come unwrapped from the livers and chestnuts, secure it with a toothpick before you fry them. The toothpick will also do for serving them.

1 lb. chicken livers	1 can (5 oz.) water chestnuts, drained
8 rashers bacon	

Cut the chicken livers in half and remove the white filaments. Cut the bacon rashers in half. Slice the water chestnuts in half vertically. Wrap the bacon round one liver and one water chestnut and fasten together with toothpick. Heat skillet and fry until bacon is browned. Makes about 16.

HAM STICKS

Buy thick ham slices or use up leftover ham for this recipe. You can either serve the ham on toothpicks or make very small sandwiches using thin whole wheat bread.

4 slices ham (about ½" thick)
2 tsp. soy sauce
2 tsp. sesame seeds, plus additional seeds for sprinkling
4 tblsp. peanut or vegetable oil
Salt and pepper

Cut the ham into 2 by 1 inch strips. Turn in mixture of soy sauce, sesame seeds, and seasonings. In skillet heat oil. Fry ham very lightly on both sides. Remove from oil, drain. Sprinkle with additional seeds and serve. Makes about 24 strips.

MUSHROOMS STUFFED WITH CRAB MEAT

This is an unusual appetizer and especially good for a small party. You can also use it for a buffet.

12 large firm, white mushrooms
½ lb. crab meat (or 7 oz. can)
2 scallions
1 tsp. dry sherry
½ tsp. ginger powder
1 tsp. cornstarch mixed with
1 tsp. water
1 egg white
Salt and pepper
¼ c. water
2 tblsp. peanut or vegetable oil
1 tblsp. soy sauce

Wash and remove stems from mushrooms. Mince crab meat and mix in bowl with finely chopped scallions, sherry, ginger, cornstarch mixture, and egg white. Season mixture and stuff mushrooms. Put in skillet, stuffed side up. Add water, oil, and soy sauce. Bring to boil and cover. Cook over low heat for 10 minutes. Drain and serve hot. Makes 12.

LUNCHEON SUGGESTIONS

The recipes in this section are chosen for their quickness and lightness, which are the prerequisites of Chinese food. Most of them require little preparation and should not be cooked until the last minute, when the diners are seated at the table.

You will find some complete Chinese dishes and some combinations of American and Chinese cooking techniques and tastes.

The chapter begins with a section on soups. Some of these are heavy enough to make a meal in themselves. Others make good starters to either dinner or lunch.

SOUP

In China soup was often drunk between courses to wash down the meal, almost in the same way that we drink water. Therefore you will find that most Chinese soups are very light and a clear bouillon forms the base. To it is added a green leafy vegetable, light dumplings, a few pieces of chicken, pork, or shrimp or perhaps egg threads. A dash of sherry will often enhance a soup but be careful with soy sauce; it can be too strong for a soup and ruin its flavor.

If you serve meat in a soup it should be added at the last minute. Never serve the meat that has been cooked for hours to form the stock. All the taste will have gone out of it into the stock. Vegetables should also be added at the last minute and should be crisp and crunchy.

Stocks should always be rich and clear, never watery. Chicken livers, giblets, skinned feet, and necks make excellent stocks. Save all bones for use in soups.

BOUILLON SOUPS

Take a clear bouillon and add a vegetable or meat to it and you'll have a Chinese soup.

Bouillon With Watercress

2 cans (10½ oz.) beef bouillon	16 pieces watercress Salt and pepper to taste

Bring bouillon to boil. Drop in watercress and boil for 1 minute. Correct seasoning and turn into heated bowls, distributing the watercress evenly. Serves 4.

Bouillon With Poached Egg

2 cans (10½ oz.) beef bouillon	4 very fresh eggs Salt and pepper to taste

Bring bouillon to boil. Drop in eggs (they must be very fresh or else the whites will string and the eggs will fall apart). When the egg is set turn into heated soup bowls. Serves 4.

2 cans (10½ oz.) beef or chicken bouillon	**Salt and pepper to taste**
1 c. shredded or finely chopped meat	

Bring bouillon to boil. Drop in meat and boil for 1 minute. Correct seasoning and turn into heated bowls, distributing the meat evenly. Serves 4.

BEEF AND VERMICELLI SOUP

Before you start making this soup marinate the beef in soy sauce and oil for half an hour. The vermicelli must be soaked in water and rinsed before it is cooked since you will not be rinsing it after cooking. You can add spinach or other green vegetable leaves to the soup at the end to make it go further.

½ lb. lean beef	Salt and pepper
1 tblsp. soy sauce	2 oz. vermicelli
1 tsp. peanut or vegetable oil	2 scallion tops
	6 c. chicken or beef stock

Chop beef into shreds and marinate in soy sauce, oil, and seasoning for half an hour. Soak vermicelli for 10 minutes in cold water. Chop scallion tops. Bring stock to boil. Drain vermicelli and add with scallions. Simmer for 5 minutes. After 2 minutes add beef and simmer for 3 minutes. Turn into heated bowl and serve. Serves 4.

CHICKEN BROTH AND CUCUMBER SOUP

This is a very good way of using up leftover chicken and produces a soup that is a meal in itself. Add 1 cup chopped chicken to the soup during the last 3 minutes of its cooking time. The soup takes only about 7 minutes to prepare.

The soup can also be improved by the addition of

61

small peeled radishes, or raw chicken, which should be added at the beginning. Lengthen cooking time in this case until chicken is done.

2 cans (10½ oz.) chicken broth	2 cucumbers
2 c. water	2 slices ginger, chopped
	Salt and pepper

Bring chicken broth and water to boil. Peel and slice cucumbers into strips, removing the seeds. Add ginger and cucumbers to soup. Season and cook for 2 minutes. Serve at once in heated bowls. Serves 4.

CHICKEN AND SPINACH SOUP

This is a big healthy soup and can almost be considered a meal in itself. Half a chicken is boiled in the soup and reserved for use later—either as cold chicken, or in one of our Chinese chicken dishes. Or you may chop it up into the soup.

Add some chicken gizzards to the broth and chop these at the end and serve in the soup. If possible add chicken necks and wings too, but remove these before serving.

½ chicken (about 2 lbs.)	3 slices ginger, cut in half
Chicken necks and wings (optional)	1 oz. vermicelli
	½ lb. spinach
Chicken gizzards (optional)	1 tblsp. dry sherry
1 onion	Salt and pepper
2 celery stalks	

Note: *Instead of water you can add 1 can (10½ ounce) chicken broth.*

Bring chicken, necks, wings, and gizzards, etc., to boil with coarsely sliced onion, celery, and ginger, with enough water to cover. Boil for 1 hour. Remove chicken from pot and add vermicelli, spinach, sherry, and seasoning. Cook until spinach is tender. Remove gizzards, and if desired, chop into small pieces, and add to soup. If desired, add chopped chicken to soup. Serve. Serves 4.

EGG DROP TOMATO SOUP

This is excellent for a winter's day, particularly when you come back from the movies or theater. It's also extremely quick and simple. You can make it while your guests are waiting.

2 cans (10½ oz.) tomato soup
2 soup cans water
2 tblsp. dry sherry

1 tsp. ground black pepper
Salt
2 eggs, beaten

Bring the soup and water to a boil, add the sherry, pepper, and salt and boil for 1 minute (to cook sherry). Remove from heat. Slowly stir the eggs into the soup until almost set. It will keep cooking almost until you're eating it so don't overcook it on the stove or it will be tough and stringy. Serves 4–6.

PORK SOUP

Use either fresh pork, added at the beginning of the soup, or leftover pork, minced and added at the end with the mustard cabbage. This soup is very good at the beginning of a small dinner. It requires almost no preparation and is simple to serve.

¼ lb. lean pork
1 celery stalk
2 scallion tops

½ lb. mustard cabbage
6 c. chicken stock
Salt and pepper

Mince the pork and chop the celery and scallion tops. Wash and chop the cabbage. Bring stock to boil and season. Add pork, celery, and scallions, and simmer for 10–15 minutes so that the pork is fully cooked. If using cooked pork simmer for 5 minutes. Add cabbage and cook for 3 minutes. Turn into heated soup bowls, distributing ingredients evenly. Serves 4.

FRESH VEGETABLE SOUP

This soup is excellent for lunch, or as the last thing at night after the theater. You can add leftover rice or noodles and leftover vegetables to it.

To drain off excess oil place a slice of bread on top of the soup while it is cooking. The bread will absorb it.

1/4 lb. cabbage	2 c. boiling water
1/4 lb. carrots	1/2 c. star noodles or left-
1/4 lb. celery	overs
2 scallions	2 tblsp. soy sauce
1 tblsp. peanut or vegeta-	1 tsp. dry sherry
ble oil	Salt and pepper
2 c. hot canned chicken	
broth	

Chop the vegetables and scallions. In pot heat oil. Fry the vegetables lightly for 1 minute. Drain off excess oil. Add hot broth and water. Simmer for 15 minutes, covered. Add noodles or leftovers and simmer for about 3 minutes. Add soy sauce, sherry, and seasoning. Simmer for 5 more minutes. Serves 4.

FISH AND SHELLFISH

Although we rarely cook fish and vegetables together, the Chinese nearly always do. Their use of ginger helps to eliminate the fishy taste.

Lobster, shrimp, oysters, and other shellfish also play an important part in the Chinese kitchen. We have used Chinese techniques in cooking American seafood (such as steamed clams) as well as straightforward Chinese recipes. The fast cooking and the spices used prevent toughening and bring out the aroma of the seafood.

PEANUT FISH CAKES

For this recipe use any white fillet of fish such as sole, flounder, or haddock. You will need a blender to grind the ingredients, otherwise it will take you hours to chop everything up.

Serve the fish cakes with an avocado salad. Some dips set on the table would also make the meal more interesting; for example, Hot Mustard*, soy sauce, Oyster Sauce*, Sweet and Sour Sauce*. Check Index for these or buy them bottled.

1 lb. fish fillets	1 tblsp. soy sauce
¾ lb. raw shrimp	1 egg white
4 slices smoked bacon, cooked	2 tblsp. cornstarch
	Salt and pepper
1 c. peanuts	1 c. peanut or vegetable oil
1 tsp. powdered mustard	

Wash the fish and shell and devein the shrimp. Add to the blender with the bacon and peanuts. Grind finely. Blend in mustard, soy sauce, egg white, cornstarch, and seasoning. Make the mixture into patties. In skillet heat oil. Fry patties on both sides until brown. Cover and cook for 3 minutes. Drain on paper towels. Serve hot. Serves 4.

POACHED FISH FILLETS

Here is a new and extremely simple way of poaching any white fish fillet (sole, flounder, etc.). It makes a delicious luncheon course, or a good dinner course served with mashed potatoes and a green vegetable.

4 fresh fish fillets (about 2 lbs.)	2 tblsp. peanut or vegetable oil
2 slices fresh ginger, chopped (or 1 tsp. powdered)	2 scallions, chopped
	2 tblsp. soy sauce
Water to cover fish	Salt and pepper

Preheat oven to low temperature, about 250° F. In skillet place fish and ginger. Cover with water and bring to boil. Turn down heat and simmer for about 5 minutes. The fish is done when it is flaky. When it is cooked remove from pan and place in a low oven in a heated dish to keep warm. Empty water from skillet and heat oil. Stir-fry scallions for 2 minutes. Add soy sauce and seasoning. Pour over fish and serve. Serves 4.

CHINESE STEAMED CLAMS

Here are two different ways of steaming clams Chinese style. You may either serve the clams immediately after steaming, or proceed to the next step of pan-frying them in the traditional Chinese way. The two steaming methods produce a completely new flavor.

You can serve this either as a starter to a dinner, or as a main luncheon course. You might pan-fry them and serve them over noodles or rice.

Clams Steamed in Sherry

3 dozen fresh clams
1 c. dry sherry
Water to cover

1 onion, coarsely sliced
Pepper

Bring sherry and water to boil. Add the clams and enough extra water to cover them. Add the onion and pepper to taste. Cover and steam them until the shells open. Serves 4.

Clams Steamed in Broth

3 cups chicken broth
3 doz. fresh clams
Water to cover
2 cloves garlic, crushed

2 tblsp. peanut or vegetable oil
Pepper

Bring broth to boil. Add clams and enough water to cover them. Add garlic, oil, and pepper. Cover and steam until the shells open. Serves 4.

FRIED CLAMS

3 doz. shelled steamed clams	2 tblsp. white wine or dry sherry
2 tblsp. peanut or vegetable oil	2 tblsp. cornstarch mixed with
1 clove garlic, crushed	2 tblsp. water
2 tblsp. soy sauce	½ c. chicken broth
2 tblsp. sugar	Salt and pepper
2 tblsp. vinegar	2 tblsp. chopped parsley

Shell clams after steaming, using either of the preceding methods. In skillet heat oil. Add garlic and stir-fry 1 minute. Add clams, stir-fry 1 minute. Add soy sauce, sugar, vinegar, and white wine. Bring to boil. Add cornstarch mixture. Heat broth and add. Season and cook for about 5 minutes, until the sauce is thick enough to coat the spoon. Sprinkle with parsley and serve. Serves 4-6.

CELERY HEARTS WITH CRAB MEAT

Serve this dish over rice and save the green part of the scallions to scatter over the top for decoration. Although we use only the heart of the celery here, the rest can be saved for future use in soups or stocks, so nothing is wasted.

2 bunches celery (use heart)	1 tblsp. soy sauce
3 tblsp. peanut or vegetable oil	1 tblsp. dry sherry
	½ c. chicken stock
1 clove garlic	1 tblsp. cornstarch mixed with
2 scallions	1 tblsp. water
½ lb. crab meat or 1 can (7 oz.), drained	Salt and pepper

Parboil the celery hearts for 3 minutes. Drain and

dry. Heat oil in skillet. Crush the garlic, chop the scallions, and fry for 1 minute (use only the white part of the scallions). Add celery. Fry for 2 minutes. Add the crab. Fry for 3 minutes. Add soy sauce, sherry, and chicken stock. Bring to boil. Add cornstarch mixture and season. When sauce is thick enough to coat spoon, remove from heat and serve. Serves 4.

PEPPERS STUFFED WITH CRAB MEAT

These peppers can be served with a salad for a luncheon, or with a buffet dinner. To make them more attractive sprinkle a little paprika over them before you serve them.

4 large green peppers	Salt and pepper
½ lb. crab meat or 1 can (7 oz.), drained	2 tblsp. peanut or vegetable oil
1 c. cooked rice	½ c. chicken stock
1 egg, beaten	1 tblsp. soy sauce
½ tsp. ginger powder mixed with	
½ tsp. dry sherry	

Wash, cut the peppers and remove seeds, scrape out their insides. In a bowl mix together crab meat, rice, egg, and ginger-sherry mixture. Season and stuff into pepper halves. In skillet put oil, stock, and soy sauce. Bring to boil, add peppers, cover and cook for about 20 minutes, until the peppers' skins are cooked. Serves 4.

CHINESE FRIED OYSTERS WITH BACON

This dish can be served with rice for lunch, or as an hors d'oeuvre using the sauce as a dip. You can also use a variety of other sauces as dips too, such as Duk Sauce*, soy sauce, Sweet and Sour Sauce*, etc.

Wrap the oysters with the bacon and skewer with a toothpick if the bacon seems to be unwrapping itself from the oyster. To serve, spoon the sauce over the oysters.

2 doz. oysters	1 tsp. soy sauce
12 rashers bacon	1 tblsp. cornstarch mixed
2 eggs	with
1 large onion	1 tblsp. water
3 dried Chinese	2 tblsp. chicken stock
mushrooms, soaked in	2 tblsp. peanut or vegeta-
water overnight (or for	ble oil
30 min.)	Salt and pepper

Shell the oysters. Cut the bacon strips in half and wrap around the oysters. Beat the eggs and dip the wrapped oysters in them. Chop the onion finely. Drain and chop the mushrooms; preserve their soaking liquid. Blend together soy sauce, cornstarch mixture, stock, and mushroom liquid. Heat oil in skillet. Sauté the oysters until browned on all sides. Remove and drain. Pour off half the fat. Add onions and stir-fry for 2 minutes. Add mushrooms and stir-fry for 1 minute. Add soy sauce mixture. Bring to boil. When sauce coats spoon, season and pour over oysters. Serve at once. Serves 4.

SMOKED OYSTERS WITH STRING BEANS

This dish is a little more exotic and makes a good, light luncheon dish. Again, it's extraordinarily simple to prepare. Hint on cooking frozen string beans: don't add any water. Just cover and let simmer over *very* low heat until they are done.

You can also serve this cold as a salad. Just pour 2 teaspoons oil over beans and serve when cold.

1 pkg. (10 oz.) frozen str-	2 cans (3¾ oz.) smoked
ing beans (or 1 lb.	oysters
fresh)	3 scallions, sliced
2 tblsp. peanut or vegeta-	2 tblsp. soy sauce
ble oil	Salt and ground pepper

Simmer beans in water to cover until tender (about 20 minutes). Drain. Heat skillet, add oil; when it is hot add oysters. Stir for 2 minutes. Add beans and scallions. Cover for 2 minutes. Add soy sauce, season, and serve in heated dish. Serves 4.

SCALLOPS WITH STRING BEANS

Use bay scallops. If you can only get the ocean ones cut them in half.

To make an attractive meal, serve the scallops over Spanish rice. Add different color peppers to the rice for effect. These can be baked in the oven in a greased baking dish for 30 minutes and then chopped into the rice. Here you will be adopting the Chinese attitude to color in food, if not the Chinese style.

1 lb. scallops	½ c. peanut or vegetable oil
½ c. dry sherry	2 tblsp. soy sauce
1 lb. string beans or 1 pkg. (10 oz.) frozen	1 c. chicken stock
	Salt and pepper

Marinate scallops in sherry for at least 2 hours. Chop the string beans into 2 inch pieces and parboil. If frozen, thaw but do not parboil. Dry thoroughly. Drain and dry scallops. In skillet heat oil. Quick-fry the scallops over medium heat for 10 minutes until three-quarters cooked. Remove to heated dish. Add string beans to pan. Stir-fry for 2 minutes. Add soy sauce, stock, and seasoning. Cover and cook over medium heat until the beans are almost cooked. Return the scallops to the pan and cook for 5 minutes. Serve immediately. Serves 4.

SPICY SHRIMP WITH PICKLED VEGETABLES

Serve this for lunch on whole wheat toast.

Use your imagination in choosing the pickled vegetables. Try different types: hot cauliflower, pimiento, white radishes, Kosher pickles, or relish. The different shapes, sizes, colors, and tastes will make the dish unusual and interesting.

1 lb. raw shrimp	½ c. dry sherry
2 scallions	1 c. chicken stock
3 slices ginger	1 tblsp. soy sauce
1 garlic clove	½ tsp. brown sugar
1 fresh cucumber (optional)	2 tsp. cornstarch mixed with
3 tblsp. peanut or vegetable oil	2 tsp. water
	Salt and pepper
3 tblsp. chopped varied pickled vegetables (leave the small ones —e.g. cauliflower—whole)	2 tsp. fresh chopped dill (optional)

Shell and devein the shrimp. Chop scallions, ginger, and crush garlic. Peel and slice cucumber. In skillet heat oil. Add scallions, ginger, and garlic. Stir-fry for 2 minutes. Add shrimp and stir-fry for 2 minutes. Add vegetables and sherry. Remove shrimp to a side dish. Add chicken stock, soy sauce, sugar. Bring to boil and add cornstarch mixture. When sauce coats spoon, return shrimp to pan, heat through, season, scatter dill over top and serve. Serves 4.

MEAT AND POULTRY

Prepare these dishes by doing all the necessary chopping in advance. The cooking time for most of them is about 15 minutes. Don't start cooking until the diners are seated at the table.

In these recipes the meat and vegetables are cooked together in the traditional Chinese way. The proportions given are larger than the Chinese, because they form complete dishes. You can make a meal interesting by cooking two dishes at once, using half the amount given in each recipe.

GROUND BEEF WITH CHINESE VEGETABLES

Hamburgers can be excellent only when they are made with good meat. It's the best to get the butcher to grind it in front of you. You should not use meat that is too fatty.

Serve hamburgers with peas and potatoes.

1 lb. ground beef
1 can (5 oz.) bean sprouts, drained
1 can (5 oz.) water chestnuts, drained

2 tblsp. soy sauce
Salt and pepper
1 tblsp. flour
3 tblsp. peanut or vegetable oil

Place ground beef in mixing bowl. Chop bean sprouts and water chestnuts finely. Add to bowl with soy sauce. Mix together, season. Make into 4 hamburgers and roll in flour. In skillet heat oil. Sauté hamburgers on both sides for 2-3 minutes or longer depending on how you like them done. Serves 4.

CHINESE AVOCADO SALAD AND STEAK

Here we've combined steak and salad to make a delicious light luncheon. If you can buy fresh ginger, fry the steak of your choice in peanut or vegetable oil with ginger slices. Serve it with the slices and chopped scallions on top of it. With it we have an avocado salad with a Chinese dressing.

Avocado Salad

2 large ripe avocados
2 ripe red tomatoes

1 onion

Dressing

2 tblsp. peanut or vegetable oil
1 tblsp. soy sauce

1 tsp. rosemary
Salt and pepper

Peel, pit, and chop the avocados and tomatoes into slices. Shred the onion. Place in bowl. Mix dressing, pour over, and serve. Serves 4.

STEAK AND ASPARAGUS

This is an economical dish because you can buy an inexpensive cut of steak. The meat does not toughen when it is shredded and cooked in this Chinese way.
Serve the meal with grilled tomatoes and noodles.

1 lb. chuck steak	1 clove garlic
1 lb. asparagus or 1 pkg. (10 oz.) thawed frozen	1 tsp. salt
	½ c. stock
1 red onion	1 tblsp. cornstarch mixed with
1 pimiento	1 tblsp. water
4 tblsp. peanut or vegetable oil	Pepper

Cut the steak into thin strips, against the grain. Slice the asparagus into 1½ inch sections, discarding the hard white part if it is fresh and parboil. Shred the onion and slice the pimiento finely. In skillet heat oil. Crush garlic and add to pan. Salt and stir-fry for 1 minute. Add onion, stir-fry for 1 minute. Add pimiento and steak. Brown the meat. Add asparagus and fry for 1 minute. Then pour in stock. Bring to boil and simmer for 5 minutes. Add cornstarch mixture. Cook until sauce coats spoon. Season and serve. Serves 4.

CHICKEN WITH ASPARAGUS

This is a very quick meal if you use thawed frozen asparagus instead of fresh, which takes much longer to cook. Serve it with rice and either grilled tomatoes or a tomato salad.

1 pkg. (10 oz.) thawed frozen asparagus	½ tsp. Tabasco sauce
4 chicken breasts, boned	1 c. boiling chicken stock
3 tblsp. peanut or vegetable oil	1 tsp. cornstarch mixed with
1 tsp. dry sherry	1 tsp. water
1 tsp. soy sauce	Salt and pepper

Slice asparagus and dry on paper towels. Pound and slice chicken breasts into 1 inch cubes. In skillet heat oil. Add chicken and stir-fry for 3 minutes. Add asparagus and cook for 3 minutes. Pour in sherry, soy sauce, Tabasco, and boiling stock. Cook for 2 minutes. Add cornstarch mixture, season, and cook until sauce coats the spoon. Serve immediately. Serves 4.

CHICKEN AND NOODLES

This is another 10 minute luncheon dish. If you have time, though, let the chicken strips marinate for a couple of hours in the mixture described. You can serve it with a salad, or perhaps braised zucchini, broccoli, spinach—almost any green vegetable would go well with it. When you are cooking chicken breasts pound them first. This breaks the little blood vessels and makes the chicken more tender and juicy.

4 chicken breasts, boned	1 c. egg noodles
½ tsp. grated ginger	1 qt. boiling water
2 tsp. dry sherry	1 c. hot chicken stock
1 tsp. plus 3 tblsp. peanut or vegetable oil	½ tsp. cornstarch mixed with
1 clove garlic, finely chopped (or squeezed through a garlic press)	1 tsp. water
	½ tsp. soy sauce

Cut the raw chicken breasts into thin strips. In a bowl mix the ginger, sherry, 1 teaspoon oil, and garlic.

Turn the chicken breasts in the mixture. Leave to marinate if there is time. When ready drop noodles into boiling water and cook for 3-4 minutes. Rinse under cold tap (to stop them from cooking and remove starch). Heat skillet; add remaining oil. When hot add chicken and cook for 3 minutes, stirring constantly. Add hot chicken stock and cook for 1 more minute. Stir in blended cornstarch and soy sauce and cook for 2 minutes. Place noodles in heated dish, pour chicken mixture over, and serve. Serves four.

RED-STEWED CHICKEN LEGS

This dish takes about an hour and a half to cook, but it can be prepared ahead of time and reheated before serving. The legs are red-stewed, meaning that they are stewed with soy sauce, and served with vegetables and rice. You may use leftover vegetables instead of the peas. Add them at the end.

6 chicken legs	1 tblsp. dry sherry
½ can (5 oz.) bamboo shoots	4 tblsp. soy sauce
1 leek	1 tsp. sugar
4 tblsp. peanut or vegetable oil	½ pkg. (10 oz.) frozen green peas or leftover vegetables, diced
3 slices ginger, chopped	Salt and pepper
2 c. chicken stock	

Dry chicken legs on paper towels. Drain bamboo shoots. Thoroughly clean, wash, and dry leek. Chop into half inch pieces. In skillet heat oil. Add ginger and leek and stir-fry for 1 minute. Add chicken legs and brown on all sides. Add bamboo shoots and fry for 1 minute. Meanwhile bring stock to boil in another saucepan. To skillet add sherry, soy sauce, and stock. Bring to boil and add sugar. Cover and simmer for half an hour or until the juices of the legs run clear and yellow when pierced by a fork. Add peas in last 15 minutes of cooking time. Season and serve. Serves 4.

Note: *When using frozen vegetables, such as peas, slice off the desired amount with serrated knife and put the rest back in the freezer.*

CHICKEN AND MUSHROOMS

Don't start cooking this until you are ready to eat. Have everything chopped and ready on a plate. Choose large juicy chicken breasts and pound them before you chop them.

Serve with rice or noodles and a salad.

4 chicken breasts, boned	1 onion, chopped
1 tsp. ginger powder	4 tblsp. peanut or vegetable oil
1 tsp. dry sherry	
1 tsp. cornstarch mixed with	1 clove garlic, crushed
1 tsp. water	1 c. boiling chicken stock
Salt, pepper	1 tsp. soy sauce
4 dried Chinese mushrooms, soaked in water overnight (or for 30 min.)	1 tsp. sugar
	Salt and pepper

Pound and slice chicken breasts into 1 inch pieces. Place in bowl and cover with ginger powder, sherry, cornstarch, and seasoning. Drain and chop mushrooms. Reserve soaking liquid. Chop onion. In skillet heat oil. Stir-fry garlic and onion for 1 minute. Add chicken and mushrooms and cook for 4 minutes. Add boiling stock, soy sauce, sugar, and seasoning. Cook until sauce is thick and coats spoon. Serve immediately. Serves 4.

CHICKEN LIVERS AND NOODLES

For this dish buy the wide flat noodles. It's a good winter luncheon dish if you serve it with a red wine—

perhaps an Italian one—and hot, fresh Italian bread. You might serve a salad, or grilled mushrooms and tomatoes. Don't forget to rinse the noodles immediately in cold water when you're cooked them.

8 ozs. flat noodles
1 qt. boiling water
1 container chicken livers (about 2 lbs.)
3 tblsp. peanut or vegetable oil
1 clove garlic, crushed
3 slices ginger, chopped (or 1 tsp. powdered)

1 onion, thinly sliced
½ c. chicken stock
2 tblsp. sherry
1 tsp. soy sauce
1 tsp. cornstarch mixed with
1 tsp. water
Salt and ground pepper

Preheat oven to 250° F. Drop noodles into boiling water and cook for 8 minutes. Meanwhile slice the livers, removing the white filament. When noodles are ready rinse in cold water, drain. Heat skillet, add 1 tablespoon oil and when hot, fry garlic and ginger. Add the noodles. Fry for 2 minutes. Remove to a hot serving dish and keep warm in oven.

Wipe pan and add 2 tablespoons oil. Fry onion for 1 minute, then add livers. Stir rapidly for 2 minutes. Add stock, sherry, soy sauce, cornstarch mixture, and seasoning. Stir for 2 more minutes. When ready pour over noodles. Serves 4-6.

SKEWERED CHICKEN LIVERS AND SAUSAGES

This makes an excellent dish either for a luncheon or for a barbecue. The ingredients are threaded on a skewer and marinated for an hour before they are cooked. They are then grilled for about 15-20 minutes.

Dip the mixture in a barbecue sauce, or choose one of the Chinese sauces listed in the Index.

2 lbs. chicken livers
18 rashers bacon
2 cans (5 oz.) water chestnuts, drained
4 green peppers

1 lb. baby link sausages
½ c. soy sauce
1 tblsp. honey
¼ c. dry sherry
Salt and pepper

Trim the livers, removing any white filament. Cut in half. Cut bacon rashers in half and wrap around liver. Cut the chestnuts in half, vertically. Half and quarter the peppers. Thread all the ingredients, plus the sausages, in different order along skewers. You will probably need about 12. In a bowl mix together the soy sauce, honey, sherry, and seasoning. Marinate the ingredients on the skewers for an hour. Heat grill and cook, turning frequently, for 15-20 minutes. Serves 6.

PAN-STIRRED CHICKEN HEARTS AND GIZZARDS

This is an excellent, quick, and economical luncheon dish. We suggest you serve it with grilled tomatoes and rice. While the latter two are cooking do all the necessary chopping and slicing for the main dish.

Put the rice, encircled with the grilled tomatoes, on a serving dish in the oven to keep warm while you cook the hearts and gizzards. This way you'll have no trouble with timing. When the mixture is cooked, pour it over the rice and serve. Everything will be on the one dish.

1 lb. mixed chicken gizzards and hearts
2 tblsp. peanut or vegetable oil
3 scallions, chopped
3 stalks celery, finely chopped
½ cabbage, shredded
2 tblsp. soy sauce

Trim the chicken gizzards by removing the outside filaments and slice thinly. Cut the hearts in half. Heat skillet, add oil, and when it is hot, toss in the hearts and gizzards. Cook for 2 minutes, stirring constantly. Add scallions, celery, and cabbage. Stir, cover, and cook for 2 more minutes. Add soy sauce and stir for another minute. Serves 4.

COLD FRIED CHICKEN CHINESE-STYLE

This can be eaten hot or cold for luncheon and goes very well with salads. The trick when frying chicken is to listen to the sound of the fat. When it spits and crackles, without smoking too much, it is ready for the chicken. Drop in a piece of bread—if it sizzles straight away, the fat is hot enough.

4 chicken breasts

Coating

1 egg	Salt and pepper
1 tsp. dry mustard	½ c. bread crumbs
1 tsp. curry powder	½ c. peanut or vegetable
1 tsp. soy sauce	oil

Mix together egg, mustard, curry powder, soy sauce, seasoning. Remove chicken bones. Dip chicken in egg mixture. A useful hint—fill a plastic bag with the bread crumbs and shake the chicken around in it. Heat oil. Sauté the chicken in the oil til brown and juices run clear and yellow when pierced with a fork. Serves 4.

BRAISED EGGPLANT WITH BACON AND TOMATO

Serve this quick luncheon dish over rice. It's ideal for a winter meal. You might choose a red wine to go with it.

Peel the tomatoes by dropping them into boiling water. Cube the eggplant and let it stand for an hour, salted, to get rid of the excess moisture. Dry thoroughly on paper towels before cooking.

8 strips smoked bacon	2 slices ginger, chopped
4 tomatoes	1 eggplant, cubed
2 cloves garlic	Salt and pepper

Brown the bacon, after cutting into 2 inch strips. Remove and drain. Peel, seed, and quarter the tomatoes. Crush garlic and add to bacon dripping in pan with ginger. Stir-fry for 1 minute. Add eggplant cubes to pan. Fry over high heat for 2 minutes, browning all sides. Turn down heat and add tomatoes. Season, cover, and cook for 15-20 minutes, or more, until eggplant is done. Add bacon to mixture and serve. Serves 4.

CALF'S LIVER WITH VEGETABLES

This is a quick and easy luncheon dish. It will stretch to 4 people and uses very little liver. Serve it with rice and perhaps a glass of beer to go with it.

—A hint on rolling meat in flour before frying: put the flour in a plastic bag, put in the meat, and shake it around. It's so much easier and less messy.

1 lb. calf's liver	1 onion, finely sliced
2 tblsp. dry sherry	½ pkg. (10 oz.) frozen
2 tblsp. soy sauce	snow peas, thawed
1 slice ginger, chopped (or ½ tsp. powdered)	1 bell pepper, finely chopped
⅓ c. flour	Salt and ground pepper
⅔ c. peanut or vegetable oil	

Chop liver finely. In bowl mix sherry, soy sauce, ginger. Leave liver to marinate for at least 15 minutes, 2 hours if possible. Dry the liver and coat with the flour. Heat the skillet, add the oil, and when hot sauté the liver very lightly on both sides until it is brown. Remove to hot dish. (You want to make sure you do not overcook the liver, but at the same time the flour must be cooked.) Add the onion, snow peas, and pepper. Cook for 2 minutes, stirring constantly. Pour over liver, season, and serve. Serves 4.

FRIED PORK WITH CLAMS

Serve this with saffron rice or Fried Rice*.

Steam the clams in Chinese sherry broth. See Clams Steamed in Sherry*.

You may use leftover pork here, which you would add to the pan at the end instead of the beginning. You can also add chopped leftover vegetables.

3 doz. clams	1 onion
½ c. clam broth	½ lb. fresh mushrooms
1 tblsp. cornstarch mixed with	½ lb. pork
1 tsp. water	3 tblsp. peanut or vegetable oil
2 tblsp. soy sauce	Salt and pepper

Steam clams, shell them, and reserve half a cup of broth. In bowl mix broth with cornstarch mixture and soy sauce. Add clams and toss. Leave in mixture. Chop onion and mushrooms finely. Shred pork against the grain. In skillet heat oil. Add pork and fry for 3 minutes. Add onion and mushrooms. Stir-fry for 2 minutes. Add clams and soy sauce mixture. Bring to boil. When sauce coats spoon remove from pan, season, and serve. Serves 4.

FRIED PORK WITH ZUCCHINI AND CUCUMBER

Serve this dish with garlic bread and a hot potato salad. Add half a teaspoonful of Chinese Hot Mustard* to the salad dressing.

For variety we've combined zucchini and cucumber in the same dish. Peel them and run the prongs of a fork down their sides. When you slice them it will have a lacy effect.

1 lb. pork	2 tblsp. peanut or vegetable oil
1 tblsp. soy sauce	1 c. chicken stock
1 cucumber	Salt and pepper
1 zucchini	
½ can (5 oz.) bamboo shoots (optional)	

Note: *You may also use yellow squash in this dish.*

Slice the pork thinly against the grain. In bowl toss the meat in soy sauce and let stand while you chop peeled cucumber and zucchini. Drain bamboo shoots. In skillet heat oil. Dry pork and stir-fry for 4 minutes. Add vegetables and stir-fry for 2 minutes. Add chicken stock, cover and cook over medium heat until vegetables and pork are done. Season and serve. Serves 4.

SHREDDED PORK WITH CHILI PEPPERS

The joy of this dish lies in the variety of colors you can introduce with the peppers. Choose, in addition to the red chili peppers, the dark green bell ones, the light green, yellow, and orange-red ones.

You can use fresh pork or leftover pork, which you add to the dish at the end.

1 lb. pork, diced	1 hot pepper
3 tblsp. soy sauce	2 chili peppers
3 tblsp. white wine	3 peppers (varying colors)
1 tsp. Tabasco sauce	1 cucumber, peeled and
1 clove garlic, crushed	diced
1 tsp. ginger powder	3 c. peanut or vegetable oil

Marinate the pork in the soy sauce, wine, Tabasco, garlic, and ginger powder. Chop the peppers and cucumber. After pork has marinated for half an hour, heat oil in skillet. Reserve marinade, dry the pork, and fry for 5 minutes, stirring constantly. Remove from pan. Add the peppers and cucumber a little at a time. Fry for 5 minutes. Remove, and return pork to pan with marinade. Cover and cook until pork is done. Add peppers and serve. Serves 4.

Note: *The oil can be saved for use in future meat dishes.*

FRIED VEAL WITH SWEET PEPPERS

The veal should hardly be cooked at all since it quickly becomes dry and stringy. Cook it just enough to change its color and serve immediately over rice.

1 lb. veal, shredded	Salt and pepper
1 tblsp. soy sauce	6 sweet peppers (you can
1 tblsp. sherry	vary this by using 3
1 tsp. cornstarch mixed	green and 3 sweet)
with	6 tblsp. peanut or vegeta-
1 tsp. water	ble oil

Marinate veal in soy sauce, sherry, cornstarch mixture, and seasoning. Leave to stand for 15 minutes. Chop peppers into 1 inch squares. Heat oil in skillet. Stir-fry peppers for 3 minutes. Remove from pan. Add veal and stir-fry for about 1 minute, until it changes color. Return peppers to pan, correct seasoning and serve immediately. Serves 4.

EGGS

Eggs are the most versatile of foods and can be presented in a variety of different ways. The Chinese have endless different methods of producing them, from eggs boiled in tea to egg foo yung.

In keeping with the practice of never cooking one ingredient alone, the Chinese combine the eggs with other ingredients, whether meat, seafood, or vegetables. This is an excellent way to use up leftovers, or to produce a luncheon dish in a few minutes.

Save egg whites for soufflés and Chinese batters; save the yolks for egg shreds or for hot soups.

SCRAMBLED EGGS

The eggs should be stirred over gentle heat until they are just cooked. They should never be overcooked or they become dry and tasteless. Never beat in any ingredients that might produce water (such as tomatoes) before you cook the eggs, since this will make them watery. To make eggs extra good, add a little chopped butter toward the end. This will stop them cooking and make them taste richer. (Of course, the Chinese don't use butter, but this is good to know when you're cooking eggs the Western way.)

To enrich scrambled eggs further, diminish the amount of egg whites you use. As has been said, save these for use later in a Chinese batter or soufflé.

The eggs must be served the minute they are cooked or they will become leathery. In this sense they are similar to Chinese foods.

If you are scrambling the eggs in vegetable or peanut oil, the Chinese way, use a higher heat than you would use for butter-scrambled eggs. The oil won't burn them. If the heat is too low the eggs will be greasy.

SCRAMBLED EGGS WITH CRAB MEAT AND CHINESE VEGETABLES

Here's a quick lunch dish which is especially good for entertaining. Serve it with fresh Italian or French bread, and perhaps a light white wine or beer.

1 can (5 oz.) water chestnuts
1 can (5 oz.) bamboo shoots
1 can (7 oz.) crab meat, drained
4 tblsp. peanut or vegetable oil
¼ c. soy sauce
1 tblsp. dry sherry mixed with
½ tsp. cornstarch
½ c. chicken stock
Salt and pepper
6 eggs
1 tblsp. butter

Drain the water chestnuts and bamboo shoots. Chop crab meat and water chestnuts. In skillet heat oil. Sauté the vegetables for 1 minute and add crab meat. In cup mix soy sauce, sherry-cornstarch mixture, stock, and seasoning. Add to skillet, stir and let simmer until mixture thickens to coat spoon. In another pan scramble the eggs in the butter. When they are almost set fold the crab meat mixture into eggs and serve. Serves 4.

SCRAMBLED EGGS WITH SPINACH

It is well known that eggs and spinach are a most delicious combination. This dish is very simple to prepare and should be served at once, so don't start it unless the diners are seated at the table.

If you use frozen spinach, thaw it out over low heat in a separate pan, and drain off as much liquid as you can.

1 lb. or 1 pkg. (10 oz.) frozen spinach	6 tblsp. peanut or vegetable oil
6 eggs	½ tsp. soy sauce
Salt and pepper	Pinch nutmeg

Either wash and dry spinach or thaw out frozen spinach. Beat eggs and season. In skillet heat half the oil. Scramble the eggs lightly and remove to side dish. Add rest of oil, heat, and add spinach. Fry for 1 minute, or until tender. Add soy sauce, seasoning and nutmeg. Fold in eggs and serve immediately. Serves 4.

SCRAMBLED EGGS WITH WATER CHESTNUTS OR BAMBOO SHOOTS

We suggest you serve this simple dish on thin brown toast. You could perhaps serve some bacon with it, too, and grilled tomatoes to make it into a full meal.

6 eggs	2 tsp. soy sauce
1 can (5 oz.) water chestnuts or bamboo shoots, drained and sliced very small	Salt and pepper 2 tblsp. peanut or vegetable oil

Beat eggs. Add chestnuts and soy sauce. Season. In skillet (or omelet pan) heat oil; add egg mixture. Stir with a fork until the eggs are about set. Don't overcook scrambled eggs. Serves 4.

EGG STIRRED CRAB MEAT WITH MINCED PORK

A salad would go well with this dish. You can break the rules by adding a teaspoonful of butter and a little lemon juice to the egg mixture at the end.

Use leftover pork if you have any. You can substitute almost any ground meat for the pork if you wish. The dish takes no time to cook, so don't start it until everyone is ready to eat.

6 eggs	3 slices ginger, chopped
2 scallion tops	1 can (7 oz.) crab meat, drained
1 tblsp. soy sauce	½ c. minced pork
1 tblsp. dry sherry	1 tsp. butter (optional)
½ tsp. sugar	Juice ½ lemon (optional)
Salt and pepper	
3 tblsp. peanut or vegetable oil	

Beat eggs in bowl. Chop scallion tops. Mix together soy sauce, sherry, and sugar. Season eggs (not too much salt). In skillet heat oil. Add ginger and fry for 1 minute. Add crab meat and pork. Fry for about 5 minutes, until pork is cooked. Add soy sauce mixture. Stir in eggs and turn down heat. Cook for 2 more minutes. Scatter scallions over top and serve at once. Serves 4.

PORK OMELETS

The Chinese way of making omelets is very different from the American style, which is based on the French method. The Chinese mix all the ingredients together and fry individual portions. A sauce is poured over at the end. The French on the other hand, fry the filling separately and fold it inside when the eggs are cooked. If you choose the latter, you may use butter for frying if you prefer.

A hint for making good omelets: keep one pan for omelets that you never wash, just wipe out, preferably medium size with an enamel bottom.

This is a very good way of using up leftover pork. To strengthen the flavor of the sauce you might add a teaspoonful of baby food pork purée.

6 eggs	1 tsp. sugar
¾ c. minced or finely chopped cooked pork	1 tblsp. soy sauce
2 scallions, chopped	1 tsp. baby food pork purée (optional)
1¼ c. chicken stock	1 tsp. cornstarch mixed with
Salt and pepper	
4 tblsp. peanut or vegetable oil	1 tsp. dry sherry

Beat the eggs and add to the bowl the pork, chopped scallions, ¼ cup chicken stock, and seasoning. In skillet heat oil. Divide the mixture into four, and fry four individual omelets. Remove from pan. Mix sugar, soy sauce, pork purée, cornstarch mixture and add to pan. Boil remaining stock and add to pan. Cook until sauce coats spoon. Adjust seasoning. Pour sauce over omelets. Serves 4.

OMELET WITH CHOW MEIN FILLING

This is very easy and a cheat because all you need to buy is one can of chow mein at the supermarket. It's great for a light lunch, particularly if you're in a hurry. We've added a couple of ingredients to make it spicier without any extra trouble.

1 can (1 lb.) chow mein, drained	Salt and pepper
2 tsp. soy sauce	6 eggs
1 scallion, finely chopped	2 tblsp. peanut or vegetable oil

Mix chow mein, soy sauce, and scallion. Season and heat in saucepan over low flame. Beat the eggs together; season. Heat oil in skillet; add beaten eggs. With fork pull in the cooked portions from the side. When the eggs are nearly done, but runny on top, pour in the chow mein. Fold one side of the eggs over carefully. Serve. Serves 4.

EGG-STUFFED GREEN PEPPERS

This is an easy and quick luncheon dish. It is filling, so serve a light accompaniment with it.

Soy sauce, Duk (Plum) Sauce*, or Oyster Sauce* served in small dip dishes would go very well.

4 large green peppers	½ clove garlic, crushed
8 hard-boiled eggs	1 tsp. ginger powder
¼ lb. ground pork (or chopped leftover pork)	1 tsp. peanut or vegetable oil
2 rashers bacon, cooked and chopped	Salt and pepper
1 tsp. soy sauce	2 tblsp. bread crumbs
	2 c. chicken stock

Remove tops of peppers, scrape out seeds from inside; wash and dry. Separate hard-boiled yolks and whites of eggs. Mash the yolks in with pork, chopped bacon, soy sauce, crushed garlic, ginger powder, oil, and seasoning. Chop the whites separately and add them to the mixture. Stuff the peppers with the egg mixture and top with bread crumbs. Bring stock to boil in skillet. Add peppers, cover and simmer for half an hour, until tender. Serves 4.

SHRIMP OMELET

This omelet tastes better if the shrimp filling is cooked separately beforehand. When the omelet is nearly done, but still runny on top, add the shrimp mixture.

Serve this with a cooked vegetable (broccoli or pan-fried lettuce would go well) and beer.

½ lb. shrimp
2 dried Chinese mushrooms, soaked in water overnight (or for 30 min.)
1 onion
2 celery stalks

1 tblsp. soy sauce
Salt and pepper
1 tblsp. peanut or vegetable oil
6 eggs
1 tblsp. butter

Wash, shell, and devein shrimp. Chop finely. Drain mushrooms and chop with onion, celery, and mix all ingredients together. Add soy sauce and seasoning. In skillet heat oil. Stir-fry filling for 3 minutes. Remove to side dish. Beat eggs. Heat butter in omelet pan. Add eggs, reduce heat and cook, pulling in the sides with a fork, until nearly done. Add filling, fold over, and serve. Serves 4.

SANDWICHES

The Chinese never eat sandwiches as we know them, but they are such an American favorite that it seemed essential to include them in this book. Here we suggest sandwiches with a Chinese touch, suitable either for a quick lunch or for taking on a picnic.

CHOW MEIN ON ROLL

This is a good way to use up leftover lamb, beef, or any other meat. It's also popular with children and makes a delicious and simple luncheon dish.

2	tblsp. peanut or vegetable oil	
1½	c. shredded lamb	
1	onion, shredded	
3	stalks celery, diced	
1	can (5 oz.) bean sprouts, drained	

1	tsp. cornstarch mixed with
1	tsp. water
¾	c. water
Salt and pepper	
Rolls or thick-sliced bread	

Heat oil in skillet. Sauté meat for 1 minute. Add vegetables and stir-fry for 3 minutes. Blend cornstarch mixture, water, and seasoning. Add to skillet. Bring to boil. When sauce thickens enough to coat spoon, remove from heat. Spread mixture thickly over rolls or bread and serve. Serves 6.

WATER CHESTNUTS AND BACON SAND-WICHES

These are very easy to prepare and excellent for a picnic. Wrap them in foil paper so that they'll be slightly warm if you eat them several hours later.

1 can (5 oz.) water chestnuts
8 rashers bacon

8 slices black bread
¼ lb. butter

Drain and slice the water chestnuts thinly. Fry the bacon until crisp. Immediately place on slice of bread with water chestnuts. Butter another slice of bread and place on top. Wrap in foil if for picnic. Serves 4.

CANTONESE TUNA FISH SALAD SANDWICHES

Tuna fish mixed with mayonnaise and celery has become a real bore. It's a pity there's so little imagination about this fish, which is so tasty. There are hundreds of ways to bring out the flavor, and here we've added a Chinese touch. For added taste put a raw egg yolk in the mayonnaise. Serve either as a salad, or open on dark fresh bread.

1 can (7 oz.) tuna fish
3 scallions
1 green pepper
1 can (5 oz.) bean
  sprouts, drained
¾ c. mayonnaise with raw
  egg yolk (egg yolk op-
  tional)

Salt and pepper
1 tsp. soy sauce
¼ c. chopped Chinese cab-
  bage (optional)
8 thick slices dark bread

Put tuna in bowl. Chop scallions, and pepper, very finely. Put into bowl with bean sprouts; add mayonnaise, seasoning, and soy sauce. Add cabbage if desired. Mix well and spread on thick bread slices. Serves 4.

SARDINES ON TOAST

Mash the sardines to a paste and grill them on toast until they sizzle. Squeeze lemon juice over them, sprinkle them with freshly ground black pepper, and serve at once.

2 cans (3 ¾ oz.) sardines	Salt and pepper
4 scallions	8 slices toast
1 tsp. soy sauce	Juice 1 lemon

Mash sardines in their oil, in bowl. Chop scallions and add with soy sauce. Season and spread on toast and grill. When done sprinkle with more pepper, lemon juice, and serve. Makes 8 open sandwiches.

CHOPPED LIVERWURST WITH CHINESE VEGETABLES

This mixture would be good on fresh black bread. To go with it we suggest cold beer.

½ lb. liverwurst	2 tsp. water
2 celery stalks	Salt and pepper
1 scallion	8 slices bread
1 tsp. soy sauce	
1 tsp. powdered mustard mixed with	

Chop liverwurst, celery, and scallion. Mix together in bowl with soy sauce, mustard mixture, and seasoning. Spread on bread and serve. Makes 4 sandwiches.

CHOPPED CHICKEN LIVERS
WITH BEAN SPROUTS

You can add cooked bacon to this sandwich or serve it open, on toast, with grilled tomatoes on the side.

½ lb. chicken livers
1 can (5 oz.) bean sprouts
1 scallion
2 tsp. vegetable or peanut oil

1 tsp. soy sauce
1 tsp. dry sherry
Salt and pepper
4-8 slices whole wheat toast or bread

Remove filament and chop chicken livers. Drain bean sprouts and chop scallion. In skillet heat oil. Add scallion and bean sprouts, fry for 1 minute. Add chopped livers and fry for 2 minutes. Add soy sauce and sherry. Season, cook for 1 more minute. Remove from pan and spread either on toast or bread. Makes 4 sandwiches.

SALADS

Although the Chinese were the first to discover the nutritional value of raw vegetables they have no tradition of eating salads. This was originally for reasons of hygiene—raw vegetables were not safe to eat. But instead of being cooked they were often parboiled (this kills germs, brightens the color, and makes the vegetable crisp). Then they were tossed in a dressing of soy sauce and oil.

Sesame oil is the best for a salad dressing but it is expensive. Peanut oil is a good substitute or, as said earlier, add a teaspoon of sesame to peanut oil and you will get the flavor. Never let crisp leafy vegetables sit in the oil or they will become soggy. They should be tossed and served at once. Tomatoes, on the other hand, absorb the flavor of the dressing without losing their texture.

CHINESE-STUFFED AVOCADO

One of the troubles about stuffing avocados is that there is never enough room for the mixture. Take out some of the avocado meat and mix it in with the stuffing so that there is a larger area for the stuffing to fill.

Serve these with a tomato salad, or on their own. These avocados are also very decorative in a buffet.

2 large ripe avocados	Juice ½ lemon
6 dried Chinese mushrooms, soaked in water overnight (or for 30 min.)	1 tsp. curry powder
	½ tsp. Tabasco sauce
	2 tsp. peanut or vegetable oil
¼ lb. shrimp, cooked	Salt and pepper
3 tblsp. mayonnaise	Paprika
1 egg yolk	

Halve avocados and scoop out half the meat. Sprinkle with lemon to prevent browning. Place in bowl. Drain the mushrooms and dice with the shrimp. Add to avocado in bowl with mayonnaise, egg yolk, lemon juice, curry powder, Tabasco, oil, and seasoning. Mix together and fill avocados. (Sprinkle with paprika for decoration.) Serve at once. Serves 4.

BEAN SPROUTS AND HAM SALAD

Use leftover ham or ham slices. You can add chopped ginger slices, water chestnuts, cooked rice, or hard-boiled eggs to the salad for variety.

2 cans (5 oz.) bean sprouts	2 tblsp. peanut or vegetable oil
1 lb. ham	
1 stalk celery	1 tsp. sugar
2 scallions	1 tsp. powdered mustard
3 tblsp. soy sauce	

Drain bean sprouts. Chop ham into 1 inch cubes. Chop celery and scallions. Mix together soy sauce, oil, sugar, and mustard. When ready to serve combine bean sprouts, ham, celery, and scallions. Pour soy sauce mixture over ingredients, toss and serve. Serves 4.

EGG SALAD WITH WATER CHESTNUTS

This salad makes a complete course for lunch, or a side salad for a buffet. You can add different color peppers, scallions, or a chopped avocado pear for variety.

6 hard-boiled eggs	1 tsp. soy sauce
1 can (5 oz.) water chest- nuts	2 tblsp. peanut or vegeta- ble oil
1 tomato	Salt and pepper

Slice the eggs and place in a large bowl. Drain and chop the water chestnuts, chop the tomato into thin slivers; add chopped water chestnuts and tomato to bowl. Mix soy sauce, oil, and seasoning. When ready to serve, pour soy sauce mixture over other ingredients; toss and serve. Serves 3-4.

ASPARAGUS AND CHICKEN SALAD

You can use either canned or cooked fresh asparagus for this recipe. If you use fresh asparagus undercook it slightly so that it is a little crunchy.

1 can (5 oz.) asparagus or 1 lb. cooked, drained	2 tblsp. soy sauce
1 can (5 oz.) bamboo shoots	3 tblsp. peanut or vegeta- ble oil
1 tsp. sugar	1 c. chopped cooked chicken meat
½ tsp. Tabasco sauce	Salt and pepper

Chop asparagus into 1 inch pieces. Drain bamboo shoots. Mix together sugar, Tabasco, soy sauce, and oil. When ready to serve combine asparagus, bamboo shoots, and chicken. Season and toss salad with soy sauce mixture. Serves 3-4.

CUCUMBER CHICKEN SALAD

Use cooked leftover chicken or canned chicken for this salad. Fresh cooked chicken is the best; canned chicken tends to be tasteless.

Leave the cucumber to stand, salted, for about 20 minutes and dry on paper towels before you use it. This helps to get rid of the excess water. Don't pour on the dressing until you are ready to serve the salad.

2 cucumbers	½ tsp. sugar
1 tsp. salt	1 tsp. vinegar
1 clove garlic	Salt and pepper
1 tblsp. soy sauce	1 c. chopped chicken meat
3 tblsp. peanut or vegetable oil	

Peel and shred cucumber into thin strips. Salt and let stand for 20 minutes. Crush garlic and mix with soy sauce, oil, sugar, vinegar, and seasoning. When ready to serve pour soy sauce mixture over chicken and cucumber; toss and serve. Serves 3-4.

Note: *Be careful with the seasoning. Don't use too much salt—allow for the already salted cucumber and salty soy sauce.*

CHINESE TUNA FISH AND SALMON SALAD

This is a very good last-minute dish and requires little preparation. It is useful to have a couple of cans of tuna fish and salmon permanently on hand in case of unexpected guests.

1 can (7 oz.) salmon	2 tsp. peanut or vegetable oil
1 can (7 oz.) tuna fish	
1 Spanish onion	1 tsp. vinegar
1 tsp. salt	2 slices ginger, chopped
2 tsp. soy sauce	

Put the salmon and tuna fish with their juices in a

large bowl. Chop the onion finely and add. Add salt. Mix together soy sauce, oil, vinegar. Chop up ginger and add to bowl. Pour soy sauce dressing over fish mixture and toss. Serves 3-4.

CRAB MEAT AND CUCUMBER SALAD

This is an exceptionally easy and economical dish. And it's handy if you have unexpected guests for lunch. All you need to buy is a can of crab meat and two cucumbers.

A hint to make the cucumber more attractive: when you've peeled it, scrape a fork vertically along the sides of it. You'll have a pretty lacy effect on the slices.

2 cucumbers	1 tsp. vinegar
1 tblsp. soy sauce	Salt and pepper
1 tsp. dry sherry	1 can (7 oz.) crab meat,
2 tblsp. yoghurt	drained
1 tblsp. sesame oil (or pea-	
nut oil)	

Peel and slice the cucumbers as thinly as possible. Mix together soy sauce, sherry, yoghurt, oil, vinegar, and seasoning and pour over cucumbers. Let stand in the refrigerator until you are ready for it. Add the crabmeat; toss and serve. Serves 4.

DINNER MENUS

The dinner menus you find here incorporate Chinese and American dishes in one meal. You will find either a main American dish with Chinese side dishes or a main Chinese dish with American side dishes.

Check the luncheon section for soup ideas. Any of them make a good beginning to a dinner.

For vegetable ideas other than the ones listed in the menus, check the vegetable section. You will find simple Chinese methods of cooking both fresh and frozen vegetables.

As for desserts, we have not listed these separately because the Chinese rarely eat dessert. They prefer savories such as dumplings, wontons, and egg rolls. On rare occasions they might serve candied ginger, almond cookies, lichee nuts, or kumquats. Ice cream or sherbet topped with candied ginger would make an interesting dessert, or canned or fresh pineapple, fruits, or a light rice pudding.

FISH

With several thousand miles of coast, and thousands of ponds, lakes, and waterways in their country, the Chinese have always been great fish eaters. They prefer fresh-water to salt-water fish. One of the most prevalent is the carp, which is found in the rivers inland.

Westerners rarely cook fish and vegetables together, but the Chinese always do. The ginger which is cooked in the oil before the fish is added diminishes the fishy flavor.

When you buy fish, look at its eyes. They should not be sunken in the head; they should be bright as opposed to filmy and opaque. The skin should be shiny and firm, covered with scales, the gills should be red, and the tail stiff. It should smell fresh and not fishy.

Buying fish in the supermarket is not a wise thing to do since it is not always fresh. If you are buying frozen fish, check in the bottom of the packet. If there is a lump of frozen liquid you will know that the fish has been thawed and refrozen.

Keep the head on when cooking smaller fish the American way. Take the head off the larger ones. But always trim down scales and remove gills for appearance.

BRAISED COD WITH SOY BEANS

Boiled Potatoes
  String Beans

This is a very simple recipe and takes little time either to prepare or to cook. You must remember to soak the dried soy beans overnight. To give them more flavor we suggest you add salt, ginger powder, a dash of Tabasco, and a sliced onion to the water in which you soak them.

When you wash the leeks be sure to get all the grit out of them. Leeks are extremely difficult vegetables to clean.

We've suggested a fairly conventional combination of boiled potatoes and string beans to go with the dish. However, if you are feeling adventurous, consult the Index for more vegetable ideas.

BRAISED COD WITH SOY BEANS

1 c. dried soy beans soaked in water plus:	2 lbs. cleaned, sliced cod
Dash salt	2 leeks, chopped
¼ tsp. ginger powder	4 ginger slices, chopped (or ½ tsp. powdered)
¼ tsp. Tabasco sauce	½ c. dry white wine
1 onion, sliced	2 tblsp. soy sauce
¼ c. vegetable or peanut oil	1 tsp. brown sugar
	Salt and pepper

Simmer beans in soaking liquid for about ½ hour (or until tender). Heat oil in skillet. Add fish slices and fry on both sides until brown. Add chopped leeks and ginger; cook for 1 minute. Add white wine, soy sauce, brown sugar, seasoning, and beans. Cover and simmer for 15 minutes. Place on heated dish and serve. Serves 4.

BRAISED FISH STICKS

Mashed Potatoes
Peas

This is a very simple recipe and uses frozen fish sticks, which are always popular with a family. These on their own are tasteless, but this method of cooking improves their flavor. They also save you the trouble of chopping and cleaning.

We suggest peas as a vegetable since their sweetness would go well with the fish; and the traditional mashed potatoes with butter and sour cream. Add 1 tablespoon of chicken stock to the peas when you cook them.

BRAISED FISH STICKS

2 pkgs. (8 oz.) fish sticks	2 scallions
1 can (3 oz.) button mushrooms	½ c. chicken stock
	2 tblsp. soy sauce
1 can (5 oz.) bamboo shoots (optional)	1 tblsp. dry sherry
	1½ tsp. brown sugar
1 garlic clove	Salt and pepper
3 slices fresh ginger (or 1 tsp. powdered)	5 tblsp. peanut or vegetable oil

Cut fish sticks in half. Drain and slice mushrooms and bamboo shoots. Crush garlic clove. Slice ginger and scallions. In bowl mix stock, soy sauce, sherry, brown sugar, and seasoning. Heat oil in skillet. Add fish sticks and fry on both sides until golden brown. Remove and drain on paper towels. Add mushrooms, bamboo shoots, garlic, ginger, and scallions to pan. Stir-fry for 2 minutes. Add stock mixture to pan. Bring to boil. Add fish sticks and simmer for about 5 minutes. Remove from heat and serve. Serves 4.

BEAN SPROUT SAUCE*
PEAS AND SHREDDED LETTUCE

Fried or Baked Fish

When you're cooking the fish, keep the head on if it's a small one, it looks better. If you're cooking frozen fish in the oven, thaw it first, but not all the way through, and it will come out deliciously soft in the middle. Learn the difference in taste between saltwater and fresh-water fish; the fresh-water fish is

104

much sweeter. This should be a guide to the vegetables you choose.

Prepare the sauce according to the recipe listed in the Index before you cook the lettuce.

PEAS AND SHREDDED LETTUCE

2 c. chicken broth	1 c. shredded lettuce
1 lb. fresh or 1 pkg. (10 oz.) frozen peas	1 tblsp. soy sauce
	Salt and pepper

In both bring peas to boil. Cook for 2 minutes; add lettuce and cook for 2 more minutes. Remove from heat, drain. Add soy sauce, seasoning and serve. Serves 4.

FRIED FISH FILLETS CHINESE STYLE
FRIED SNOW PEAS

Baked Potato

In this recipe we keep the fish in one piece, as in Western-style cooking, but we dredge it in a Chinese way. With it we suggest a baked potato and Snow Peas, or any other green vegetable.

Since we use 2 egg whites as a coating for the fish, we suggest that you fry the yolks in oil to a very thin, well-done omelet. Slice the omelet in thin shreds and scatter them over the fish for decoration.

FRIED FISH FILLETS CHINESE STYLE

4 fresh fish fillets (about 2 lbs.)	1 tsp. water
	4 tblsp. dry sherry
2 egg whites	Salt and pepper
1 tsp. cornstarch mixed with 1 tsp. water	4 tblsp. peanut or vegetable oil

Wash and thoroughly dry the fillets. Beat egg whites and blend with cornstarch mixture and sherry.

Season. Dip fillets into mixture. Heat oil and fry fillets on both sides, until golden. Serves 4.

FRIED SNOW PEAS

3 tblsp. peanut or vegetable oil

1 pkg. (10 oz.) frozen snow peas, thawed and dried (or 1 lb. fresh)

Salt and pepper

Heat oil in skillet. Add snow peas. Fry over high heat for 1 minute. Season and stir-fry over medium heat for 3 minutes. Serves 4.

FISH WITH MANDARIN SAUCE*
BRAISED LETTUCE

Rice

This is an old classical Chinese dish and goes best with rice and a green vegetable cooked in the Chinese style. Any white fish such as cod, halibut, red snapper, sole, or trout may be used. Instead of cooking the fish whole, as the Westerner would, we cut it into small pieces. Decorate the fish with chopped scallion tops.

Prepare the Mandarin Sauce* according to the recipe listed in the Index before you cook the fish.

FISH WITH MANDARIN SAUCE*

2 lbs. fish fillets
1 egg, beaten
Salt and pepper

4 tblsp. peanut or vegetable oil
1 c. Mandarin Sauce*

Cut fish fillets into pieces 2 by 3 inches. Dip into

seasoned beaten egg. In skillet heat oil. Fry pieces on both sides until golden brown. Remove from pan and drain. Spoon Mandarin Sauce* over the fillets and serve. Serves 4.

BRAISED LETTUCE

1 firm head lettuce (any kind)	1 tsp. sugar
	2 tblsp. dry sherry
3 tblsp. peanut or vegetable oil	Salt and pepper

Slice lettuce into wide strips. Heat oil in skillet. Add lettuce and sauté for 2 minutes. Add sugar, sherry, seasoning. Stir for 1 minute. Cover and cook over low heat for 3 minutes. Serves 4.

POACHED HADDOCK

Brussels Sprouts
Boiled Potatoes

The haddock is poached in a broth with Chinese ingredients, which is then boiled down to make a sauce that we pour over the fish and serve. For decoration, if you have any leftover meat, shred about 1 dessertspoonful and scatter, with a little parsley, over the fish. We've suggested American vegetables to go with it, but you can always consult the Index for other ideas.

POACHED HADDOCK

1 tsp. vegetable or peanut oil

3 slices ginger, chopped (or 1 tsp. powdered)

2 chopped dried Chinese mushrooms, soaked in water overnight (or for 30 min.)

2 scallions, chopped

4 tblsp. shredded cabbage

4 fillets haddock (about 2 lbs.)

1 tblsp. soy sauce

1 c. chicken stock

1 tsp. cornstarch blended with

1 tsp. dry sherry

Ground white pepper to taste

Salt

1 squeeze lemon (optional)

1 tsp. finely chopped parsley (optional)

2 tsp. shredded cooked leftover meat (optional)

Heat oil in skillet. Add ginger, Chinese mushrooms, scallions, and cabbage. Stir-fry for 1 minute. Place fish fillets in pan, add soy sauce and stock. Bring to boil. Turn down heat and simmer for 10 minutes. Transfer fish to heated dish. Boil down broth to half a cupful. Add cornstarch blended with sherry. Season. If desired, add a squeeze of lemon to sauce and pour over fish. Decorate with chopped parsley and shredded meat if desired and serve. Serves 4.

DEEP-FRIED SMALL WHOLE FISH

Baked Tomatoes
Potatoes Au Gratin

Use butterfish, rockfish, or bream for this recipe. Have them cleaned but leave them whole with their heads on. Take the gills out of the top of the head for appearance.

You must marinate the fish for at least half an hour before you cook it. Fry the fish and boil down the marinade in a separate pan with a little cornstarch and use as a sauce. Serve the fish with lemon wedges and parsley to decorate.

We suggest baked tomatoes and potatoes au gratin because they can be put in the oven and almost forgotten while you prepare the fish.

DEEP-FRIED SMALL WHOLE FISH

6 small fish
4 slices fresh ginger, chopped (or 1 tsp. powdered)
3 tblsp. soy sauce
3 tblsp. dry sherry
½ tsp. anise seeds

3 c. peanut or vegetable oil
Salt and pepper
2 tsp. cornstarch mixed with
2 tsp. water
1 egg, beaten

Clean fish but leave whole removing the gills from the head. Mix ginger, soy sauce, sherry, and anise seeds in bowl. Marinate fish in the mixture for at least half an hour. Heat oil in deep pan. Combine seasoning with 1 teaspoon cornstarch and beaten egg. Dip fish into mixture and fry until golden brown. Drain on paper towels.

In another pan pour the marinade mixture. Add 1 teaspoon cornstarch. Bring to boil. Simmer until the sauce coats the spoon. Pour over fish and serve. Serves 4.

DEEP-FRIED SWEET AND SOUR FISH

Rice
Buttered Beans

Use porgie, trout, red snapper, or bass for this recipe. The fish is marinated for at least half an hour before cooking. In order for the marinade to penetrate more easily make incisions, about 2 inches apart, on the side of the fish.

Serve with Sweet and Sour Sauce*, which you can

prepare yourself very easily (see Index), or which you can buy bottled. We suggest you add chopped endive or minced scallion tops to the sauce for texture and decoration.

Rice is essential with this fish dish. Almost any green vegetable goes. Here we've suggested buttered beans for a change.

DEEP-FRIED SWEET AND SOUR FISH

2 lbs. fish	2 tsp. dry sherry
1 onion, minced	Salt and pepper
3 slices ginger, chopped (or 1 tsp. powdered)	Cornstarch for coating fish
2 tsp. soy sauce	1 c. Sweet and Sour Sauce*
	3 c. vegetable or peanut oil

Clean and scale the fish (or have your butcher do this for you). In a bowl mix minced onion, ginger, soy sauce, sherry, and seasoning. Marinate the fish in the mixture for at least half an hour. Sprinkle cornstarch over fish until it is lightly covered. At this point prepare the Sweet and Sour Sauce*. If you are using the bottled kind place in pan over low heat. Heat oil in skillet. Add fish and fry on both sides until golden brown. Drain on paper towels. Pour hot sauce over fish and serve. Serves 4.

BARBECUED SWORDFISH STEAKS

Sautéed Potatoes
  Peas

The secret's in the marinade. Although you cook these steaks the same way you normally would (over a barbecue or broiled), we suggest you marinate them first in a soy sauce-sherry mixture which you turn into a barbecue sauce afterward.

Sautéed potatoes and peas would go well with the

fish. Sauté the potatoes at the same time that you cook the fish.

BARBECUED SWORDFISH STEAKS

4 swordfish steaks (if frozen thaw and dry)

Marinade

½ c. dry white wine
¼ c. soy sauce
½ c. dry sherry
1 tsp. sugar
1 tsp. peanut or vegetable oil

1 onion, grated
Salt and pepper
2 tsp. cornstarch mixed with
2 tsp. water

Mix the marinade ingredients together in a large bowl. Place the steaks in the mixture and leave overnight if possible. Otherwise leave at least half an hour.

When ready, remove steaks from marinade and dry. While they are cooking (they take about 20 minutes) bring the marinade to a boil. Mix the cornstarch to a smooth paste with water and add to sauce. Cook until it thickens enough to coat the spoon. Pour over steaks or serve in a warm jug. Serves 4.

SHELLFISH

The Chinese have a wide variety of seafoods and their method of cooking shellfish remains one of the best. Long cooking toughens shellfish, but brief cooking time ensures that the meat is tender and aromatic.

If you buy frozen shellfish, thaw it completely before you cook it, and make sure it is wiped dry.

Crabs come in two varieties: salt and fresh water. Buy them live and rinse them in cold water. Then plunge them into boiling water. This will kill them immediately. The same applies to lobster.

Scallops should always be marinated before they are cooked and the big deep-sea scallops should be cut in half.

Shrimp plays a very important part in Chinese cooking and the deep-fried or stir-fried methods are excellent. Choose the size according to your need; the larger ones are good for deep-frying and the smaller ones for stir-frying. They should be a translucent gray color tinged with blue.

You can interchange shrimp, crab, and lobster in most of the recipes listed in this section and Lobster* or Szechwan Sauce* make good accompaniments for all.

SWEET AND SOUR CRAB MEAT BALLS

Spaghetti
  Lettuce Salad

This dish can either be served for dinner with the spaghetti and salad as we have suggested, or with a buffet.

To make the spaghetti a little different, in keeping with the Chinese way (and, in a sense, the Italian), use, instead of butter, 1 tablespoon vegetable oil and ½ clove garlic crushed with 1 teaspoon chopped parsley.

The crab meat balls are done when they rise to the surface of the oil. Although the oil for deep-frying must be sizzling hot, lower the heat when you're halfway through cooking. The temperature rises as the oil goes down.

The recipe calls for 2 tablespoons Oyster Sauce*. In this instance you might find it easier to use the bottled kind rather than making a whole batch yourself.

You can use bottled Sweet and Sour Sauce* if you don't wish to make your own. However it is very sim-

112

ple to do. You can enhance the color by adding 1 teaspoon tomato purée or ½ teaspoon red food coloring.

If you use frozen crab meat, thaw it out in the refrigerator overnight. Do not run it under the hot tap.

SWEET AND SOUR CRAB MEAT BALLS

1 lb. crab meat or 2 cans (7 oz.), drained	Salt and pepper
3 scallions, chopped	1 egg
¼ lb. fresh mushrooms	Flour to coat crab meat balls
2 tblsp. dry sherry	4 c. vegetable or peanut oil
2 tblsp. Oyster Sauce*	2 c. Sweet and Sour Sauce*

Mince crab meat with chopped scallions. Chop mushrooms and add to bowl. Add sherry, Oyster Sauce*, and seasoning. Shape the mixture into golf-ball size balls. Beat egg. Dip crab meat balls into the egg and then shake around in plastic bag with flour. (Or roll on floured board.)

Heat oil. Add the crab meat balls, a few at a time, and cook until golden brown. Drain on paper towels. Place on heated dish and pour Sweet and Sour Sauce* over them. Serve at once. Serves 4.

LOBSTER WITH CANTONESE SAUCE*

Noodles
Peas

Use fresh lobster for this recipe and cook it by plunging it headfirst into rapidly boiling water. When the shell turns a bright livid red it is done. Either scrape out the meat and spoon the sauce over it or serve the meat in the shells with the sauce served separately.

You may also parboil the lobster and finish cooking it by stir-frying the meat and adding the sauce to the pan at the end.

LOBSTER WITH CANTONESE SAUCE*

2 1½-lb. lobsters
3 tblsp. peanut or vegeta-
       ble oil
3 slices ginger, finely
       chopped

2 cloves garlic, chopped
Salt and pepper
1½ c. Cantonese (Lobster)
       Sauce*

Parboil the lobster. In skillet heat oil. Stir-fry ginger and garlic for 2 minutes. Add meat to pan, season, and cook for ten minutes. Add the sauce, bring to boil, remove from pan, and serve immediately. Serves 4.

Note: *Shrimp may be stir-fried and coated with this sauce. See Index for Stir-fried Shrimp.*

LOBSTER WITH VEGETABLES
AND FRIED NOODLES

Baked Celery

You can use frozen lobster tails for this recipe (they come about three to a package). The larger ones are better because they have more meat on them.

This is a great dish for a party. For decoration, heat the shells in the oven for a few minutes while you cook the lobster meat. Place the mixture in the shells. Arrange them spokelike over the noodles.

You'll need two pans for this recipe, one to fry the noodles in and one for the lobster and vegetables. Remember to rinse the noodles in cold water immediately after you have boiled them and remember that after frying, they will keep on cooking even after you have taken them off the flame. So be careful not to overcook them.

We suggest baked celery with this dish; it is very

simple and takes up no place on the stove. Simply place the celery in a dish with a cup of chicken broth and a tablespoon of butter. Cover with greaseproof paper, bake at about 350° F. for an hour, during which time you can prepare the ingredients for the lobster dish.

To make the table more interesting and to give flavor to the lobster, put out some dishes of Chinese Hot Mustard*, Duk (Plum) Sauce*, and soy sauce.

LOBSTER WITH VEGETABLES AND FRIED NOODLES

2 oz. rice noodles or vermicelli
4 c. chicken broth (or 1 chicken bouillon cube in 4 c. water)
1 onion
2 Chinese dried mushrooms, soaked in water overnight (or for 30 min.)
1 can (5 oz.) bamboo shoots, drained
1 green pepper
3 tblsp. vegetable or peanut oil

2 pkgs. frozen lobster tails (about 6)
2 tblsp. chopped celery
1 tsp. brown sugar
Salt and pepper
2 tsp. soy sauce
1 tsp. cornstarch mixed with
1 tsp. dry sherry
1 tsp. powdered ginger
2 c. chicken broth
1 squeeze lemon (optional)

Boil noodles in broth for 5 minutes. Drain and rinse immediately under cold water. Chop onion, drained mushrooms, bamboo shoots, and green pepper. In one skillet heat 2 tablespoons oil. Add lobster meat. Cook for 1 minute. Add chopped celery and other chopped vegetables; cook for 1 minute. Cover and cook for 2 minutes. Meanwhile, heat 1 tablespoon oil in another skillet. Add noodles. Then add brown sugar, seasoning, soy sauce, cornstarch and sherry mixture, powdered ginger, and chicken broth to lobster pan. Boil for 2 minutes. When noodles are golden, remove to heated dish. Fill shells with lobster mixture and ar-

range over noodles. Squeeze lemon over and serve.
Serves 4-6.

Note: *You can serve this dish without the shells, in
a deep dish, by spooning the mixture over the noodles.*

SWEET AND SOUR PRAWNS

Rice
Broccoli

This delicious dish would go well in a buffet but we
have listed it here since it makes a very good meal on
its own.

Never defrost prawns by running them under the
hot tap. The best way to handle them is to degut
them while they're still frozen and let them thaw out
overnight in the refrigerator.

If the sauce tastes too sour, add a little grated carrot to it, don't add more sugar. A good way to coat
the prawns with the flour: put them in a plastic bag
and shake them around in it.

SWEET AND SOUR PRAWNS

1 lb. frozen prawns (or fresh if available)
1 egg
1 tblsp. soy sauce
Flour to coat prawns
1 onion
4 tblsp. vegetable or pea- nut oil
1 clove garlic
½ tsp. ginger powder (or 4 slices fresh ginger)
¼ tsp. anise powder
2 tblsp. sugar

1 tsp. chili powder
2 tsp. dry sherry
3 tblsp. wine vinegar
2 tsp. cornstarch blended with
1 tsp. water
1 c. chicken stock
4 tblsp. chopped pineapple wedges
1 tomato, cut in wedges
1 green pepper, diced
Salt and pepper

Defrost prawns if frozen. Beat egg with soy sauce.

Dip prawns in mixture and coat with flour. Chop onion. Heat oil in skillet. Add 1 clove garlic, sliced, ginger powder, and anise powder. Add prawns and fry until golden. Remove from pan. Fry onion until clear (turn down heat). Remove garlic from pan. Add sugar, chili powder, sherry, vinegar, and cornstarch mixture. Cook for 1 minute. Add stock, bring to boil, and cook for 2 minutes. Add pineapple, tomato, and pepper. Cook for 1 minute. Add prawns. Season and serve. Serves 4.

SCALLOPS WITH STRING BEANS AND TOMATOES

Buttered Potatoes

This is a heavier meal than the scallop dish suggested in the lunch section. Boiled buttered potatoes decorated with chopped parsley would go well with it.

If the scallops are large ocean ones cut them in half so that they will cook more quickly.

Skin the tomatoes by dropping them in boiling water for 2 minutes. Cut them in half and remove the seeds.

SCALLOPS WITH STRING BEANS AND TOMATOES

¼ c. peanut or vegetable oil	1 tsp. cornstarch mixed with
1 lb. scallops	1 tsp. dry sherry
1 lb. tomatoes, skinned, seeded, and quartered	2 tsp. soy sauce
	Salt and pepper
1 lb. green beans (or 1 pkg. (10 oz.) frozen, thawed)	Juice ½ lemon (optional)

Heat oil in skillet. Add scallops. Cook for 1 minute, stirring constantly. Add tomatoes and beans. Cook for

2 minutes. Add blended sherry and cornstarch, soy sauce, and seasoning. Stir for 1 minute or until liquid thickens and coats the spoon. If desired, squeeze juice from half a lemon over before serving. Serves 4.

STIR- OR DEEP-FRIED SHRIMP
WITH SZECHWAN SAUCE*

Green Salad
   Rice

Both methods of cooking shrimp are desirable here and either will go well with Szechwan Sauce*. You can also use the dips mentioned in the buffet section, or Cantonese Lobster Sauce*.

A light vegetable, such as a green salad, is a good accompaniment.

STIR- OR DEEP-FRIED SHRIMP
WITH SZECHWAN SAUCE*

Stir-Fried Shrimp

1 lb. shrimp	1 clove garlic
3 tblsp. cornstarch	2 slices ginger
2 tblsp. dry sherry	3 tblsp. peanut or vegeta-
Salt and pepper	ble oil
1 c. Szechwan Sauce*	

Shell and devein the shrimp. Mix together cornstarch, sherry, and seasoning. Coat shrimp in the mixture and let them stand. Meanwhile prepare sauce. Mince garlic and ginger. Heat oil in skillet. Add garlic and ginger and stir-fry for 3 minutes. Add shrimp and stir-fry for about 3 to 5 minutes until done. They should be pink. Serve with sauce. Serves 4 people.

Deep-Fried Shrimp

1 lb. shrimp

Batter

4 tblsp. flour	3 tblsp. water
1 egg, beaten	Peanut or vegetable oil for
Salt and pepper	deep-frying

Shell and devein shrimp but leave their tails on.
Mix flour, egg, and seasoning. Stir in water. Dip
shrimp in batter. In skillet heat oil. When it bubbles
add the shrimp piece by piece unless you have a wire
basket. Turn the heat down to medium and cook until
shrimp are golden brown and rise to the surface.
Drain on paper towels. Serve with the sauce as a dip.
Serves 4.

CHICKEN

Chicken, along with pork and duck, is a Chinese favorite. It can be one of the most delicious of meats
since it lends itself to many flavors and varieties of
cooking. It is also an inexpensive and a simple meat to
deal with.

Be careful when buying chicken in the supermarket. Don't rush for the cheap prices and think you are
getting a bargain. You'll end up with something that
tastes like boiled bus tires. The color of the chicken is
important. It should be white, with a good firm soft
skin, not yellow and dry. You would often do better
buying a whole chicken and cutting it up for the different pieces you need. This works out much cheaper
and you also have more of an idea what you're buying.

If you buy frozen chickens (this is a bad idea; they
don't usually have much flavor since they have often
been frozen too young), thaw them out overnight in the

refrigerator. If this is impossible then put it in a bowl and leave it under a running cold tap. Never use hot water to thaw it.

The chicken is cooked when the juices run clear and yellow when pricked with a fork.

CHESTNUT CORNISH HEN

Wild Rice
String Beans in Butter

This is an unusual variation and makes an excellent dish for a dinner party. You can use an ordinary chicken in place of the Cornish hen we suggest. Serve it over wild rice with buttered string beans.

You'll need a blender to purée the chestnuts for the sauce, otherwise it takes quite some time to chop up the ingredients. To peel the chestnuts make a slit through their skins and drop them into boiling water for about 5 minutes. Peel them before they get cold or the skins will harden again and you'll be right back where you started.

Be sure to clean the leek thoroughly.

CHESTNUT CORNISH HEN

2 Cornish hens	2 c. chicken broth
5 tblsp. peanut or vegetable oil	Salt and pepper
3 slices ginger, chopped	2 lbs. chestnuts, boiled and shelled
1 leek, chopped	1 tblsp. sugar
½ c. white wine	4 tblsp. soy sauce

Clean and dry Cornish hens thoroughly. Cut in half. In skillet heat oil. Fry ginger and leek. Remove from pan and reserve. Add hens and brown. Add white wine, chicken broth, and seasoning. Cover and simmer for half an hour or until the juices run clear and yellow when the skin is pierced with a fork. Add

120

half the chestnuts and sugar. Simmer, uncovered, for another 15 minutes. In blender purée the rest of the chestnuts with soy sauce, cooked leek, and ginger. Remove hens to platter. Boil down liquid to 1 cup. Add purée. Spoon over hens and serve on bed of wild rice. Serves 4.

CHICKEN WITH ALMONDS
SAUTEED ROMAINE LETTUCE*

Rice

Chicken with nuts is a favorite combination of the Chinese and it is also easy to prepare. In keeping with the flavor of the main dish we have chosen Chinese Sautéed Romaine Lettuce* and rice.

Before you start cooking you will have to prepare the almonds. This is done by dropping them into boiling water for 2 minutes and slipping their skins while they are still warm. Dry them and bake them in a 400° F. oven with a little peanut oil until they are golden.

CHICKEN WITH ALMONDS

4 chicken breasts, boned
¼ lb. blanched, baked almonds
1 can (5 oz.) bamboo shoots, drained
1 can (5 oz.) water chestnuts, drained
1 cucumber, peeled
1 onion
3 tblsp. peanut or vegetable oil
½ c. chicken stock
1 tsp. dry sherry
½ tsp. ginger powder
½ tsp. soy sauce
½ tsp. cornstarch mixed with
1 tsp. water
Salt and pepper

Cut the chicken up into uniform squares. Place on plate with almonds. Thinly slice bamboo shoots, water chestnuts, and cucumber. Shred onion. Heat oil in skillet. Fry onion lightly for 1 minute. Add chicken and cook for 2 minutes. Add vegetables and cook for 2 minutes. Add stock, sherry, ginger powder, soy sauce. Cook for 1 minute. Add cornstarch mixture, seasoning, and cook for 2 minutes. Turn out over rice and serve. Serves 4.

SHREDDED CELERY RICE AND MUSHROOMS

Chicken Breasts

This is a delicious mixture and requires very little work. When you buy the chicken breasts choose the large ones; they won't dry up as fast as the smaller ones. Bone them and to make them more juicy pound them with the flat edge of a knife. This breaks the blood vessels inside. Add a Chinese touch by marinating them in a tablespoon each soy sauce, sherry, and chopped ginger. Then cook them whichever way you want—fried, grilled, sautéed, etc.

(You could place chicken breasts on the rice for decoration, and scatter a little parsley over the top.)

SHREDDED CELERY

3 tsp. peanut or vegetable oil	1 tsp. soy sauce
4 stalks celery, shredded	½ tsp. cornstarch mixed with
1 tsp. dry sherry	1 tsp. water
3 tsp. chicken stock	

Heat skillet. Add oil and when hot add celery. Cover, cook for 2 minutes. Add sherry, stock, soy sauce. Stir for another minute. Add cornstarch mixture and cook for 1 more minute. Empty into a heated dish. Serves 4.

RICE AND MUSHROOMS

For 4 people measure 1 cup uncooked rice. Cook rice according to directions in rice section, depending on the kind you choose, and drain. To add a bit of variety to the rice dish fry some mushrooms, thinly sliced, in a little oil and add them at the end to the cooked rice.

BEAN SPROUTS WITH GREEN PEPPERS

Broiled Chicken
  Potatoes or Rice

To give the chicken a Chinese flavor, dip it into a beaten egg mixed with herbs (thyme, rosemary, or tarragon), a teaspoon of soy sauce, and Chinese Hot Mustard*. Roll in bread crumbs and broil.

The peppers can be given a completely different flavor if you marinate them, chopped up, for an hour before. This is not essential but it does make the dish interesting.

BEAN SPROUTS WITH GREEN PEPPERS

Optional Marinade for Chopped Peppers

1 clove garlic, crushed	1 tblsp. sherry
3 tblsp. soy sauce	Juice ½ lemon

1 can (5 oz.) bean sprouts	2 tblsp. dry sherry
3 bell peppers, chopped in diagonal strips	Salt and pepper
4 tblsp. peanut or vegetable oil	

Drain sprouts and peppers (if you have marinated the latter). Heat oil in skillet. Fry peppers and sprouts for 2 minutes. Add sherry and seasoning. Cook for 1 more minute. Serves 4.

DEEP-FRIED CHICKEN WITH
RED AND GREEN PEPPERS

Rice
Lettuce Salad

This is a delicious way of frying chicken. It is chopped up into small pieces, marinated and then deep-fried with peppers. Don't get the peppers too soft—the crunchy texture, so common to Chinese foods, is essential here.

To make the cutting up of the chicken easier use sharp kitchen scissors.

With it we suggest rice and perhaps a lettuce salad. You could also consult the Index for a braised green vegetable.

DEEP-FRIED CHICKEN WITH RED AND GREEN PEPPERS

1 frying chicken cut up in small pieces

Marinade

2 tblsp. dry white wine
1 tblsp. soy sauce
4 tblsp. cornstarch
5 c. vegetable or peanut oil
4 red peppers
5 green peppers
1 clove garlic, chopped
4 slices ginger

2 tblsp. white wine
4 tblsp. soy sauce
1 tsp. Tabasco sauce
1 tsp. sugar
1 tsp. cornstarch mixed with
1 tsp. dry sherry
Salt and pepper

Marinate chicken for half an hour in wine, soy sauce, and cornstarch. Heat oil in deep skillet. Dry chicken pieces and fry until golden brown. Set aside. Chop red peppers and green peppers up into uniform pieces, about 1 inch square. Remove all but about 4 tablespoons oil from skillet. (If you are using the basket method, simply pour a little oil into another pan.) Add garlic, ginger, and peppers to pan. Fry for 2 minutes. Add chicken pieces. Pour in wine, soy sauce, Tabasco, sugar, and cornstarch-sherry mixture. Season and serve on a bed of rice. Serves 4.

BRAISED SPINACH
RICE AND PEAS

Fried Chicken

A new way to do your fried chicken: roll it in crushed-up potato chips and cooked bacon after you fry it, or roll it in Chinese Hot Mustard* and bread crumbs before frying. Allow about half an hour for the chicken to cook (we're thinking here of about 1½ pounds), so put your rice on at the same time. The spinach only takes 5 minutes, so you can leave that till the end.

BRAISED SPINACH

3 tblsp. peanut or vegetable oil
2 small onions, chopped
1 lb. spinach (or 1 pkg. (10 oz.) frozen, thawed)

2 tblsp. soy sauce
1 tsp. sugar
Salt and pepper
¼ c. boiling water
1 tblsp. cognac (optional)
Pinch nutmeg

Heat oil in skillet. Sauté onions and spinach for 5 minutes. Mix soy sauce, sugar, seasoning, and water. Pour over spinach mixture. Add cognac and pinch nutmeg; cook over low heat for 3 minutes. Correct seasoning.

Note: *Cabbage, broccoli, and celery can be cooked in the same way.*

RICE AND PEAS

1 c. washed rice	½ stick cinnamon
3 c. water	1 clove
½ lb. shelled peas (or ½ (10 oz.) pkg. frozen, thawed)	¼ c. dry sherry
	Salt and pepper

Put rice in large pot; cover with water and bring to boil. Add peas, cinnamon, clove, sherry; bring to boil. Season and simmer, covered over low heat for 20 minutes until all water has evaporated. Let stand 10 minutes after heat has been turned off.

CHINESE FRIED CHICKEN WITH BROWN SAUCE*

Brussels Sprouts
Rice

Here we have two methods for fried chicken with brown sauce. You can either fry it the American way and use the sauce for a dip, or you can use the Chinese recipe below. We suggest you cook the Brussels sprouts in the braised Chinese way if you are cooking the chicken in the American style. Prepare the Brown Sauce* before you cook the chicken.

CHINESE FRIED CHICKEN WITH BROWN SAUCE*

1 frying chicken, boned (about 2 lbs.)	½ tsp. salt
2 tblsp. dry sherry	2 c. peanut or vegetable oil
2 tblsp. cornstarch	1½ c. Brown Sauce*

Cut the chicken into small pieces about 1 by 1 inch. Dredge them with sherry, cornstarch, and salt. In skillet heat oil. Add chicken pieces and fry until golden brown. Spoon sauce over and serve. Serves 4.

FRIED CHICKEN WITH DUK SAUCE*

*Rice or Sweet Potatoes
Spinach or Broccoli*

This is quite different from the usual fried chicken we know and the sauce makes it all the more interesting. The chicken is fried in tiny pieces which you dip into the sauce. Cook your vegetables whichever way you choose; and prepare the chicken dish while these are cooking. When they are ready keep them warm in the oven while you fry the chicken. Be sure that the fat is *very hot* otherwise you will get a soggy meal.

You can either buy a can of Duk (or Plum) Sauce* or use the simple Duk Sauce recipe listed in the Index.

FRIED CHICKEN WITH DUK SAUCE*

4 raw chicken breasts	1 egg, beaten
2 cloves garlic, crushed	Salt and pepper
2 tsp. dry sherry	4 tblsp. flour
½ tsp. powdered ginger	1 c. peanut or vegetable oil

Remove bones from the chicken breasts. Pound them and slice in thin strips. Place them in a bowl and over them add garlic, sherry, ginger, beaten egg, and seasoning. Work the ingredients in. Shake flour over chicken pieces until they are thoroughly coated. (You can make this easier by putting flour in plastic bag, adding chicken pieces, and shaking them around.)

Heat skillet. Add oil and when smoking drop chicken pieces in. Fry until golden. Drain on paper towels and serve on heated dish.

FRIED ZUCCHINI

Grilled Chicken Legs
Rice

You can marinate the chicken legs before you cook them to give them a Chinese flavor. Dry them well and dust with flour, then grill.

Fried zucchini and rice make a good combination here. The zucchini has a sauce which goes well with the dry chicken.

Optional Marinade for Chicken Legs

2 tblsp. soy sauce	2 tblsp. dry sherry
1 clove garlic, crushed	Salt and pepper

FRIED ZUCCHINI

3 small, firm zucchini	1 tsp. dry sherry
2 tblsp. peanut or vegetable oil	Salt and pepper
	1 c. hot chicken stock
1 clove garlic	
1 slice fresh ginger (or 1 tsp. powder)	

Wash and slice zucchini. Heat oil in skillet. Fry garlic and ginger. Discard. Toss slices of zucchini in oil for 1 minute. Add sherry and seasoning. Cook for ½ minute. Add broth, cover and cook for 4-5 minutes. Serves 4.

PAN-STIRRED BROCCOLI

Roast Chicken
Rice

This is a very good combination and simple to arrange. You prepare the broccoli while the chicken is cooking in the oven.

A hint on the roasting of the chicken: during its last half hour baste it with heavy cream and 2 tablespoons sherry. You'll have a delicious sauce which you can strain into a warm jug. It's not, of course, Chinese, but the flavor will mix very well with the broccoli and rice.

PAN-STIRRED BROCCOLI

1 lb. broccoli	¼ tsp. sugar
2 tblsp. vegetable or pea-nut oil	Dash nutmeg
	Salt and pepper
½ tsp. powdered ginger (or 2 slices fresh)	

Slice broccoli very thin and split flowerets. Heat oil in skillet and add ginger, then broccoli. Stir and cook covered for 5 minutes, stirring occasionally. Uncover, add sugar, nutmeg, and seasoning. Serves 4.

BLACK BEAN SAUCE*
FRIED BEAN SPROUTS

Sautéed Chicken
Rice

Instead of buying a chicken that's already cut up, buy a whole chicken and cut it up yourself. It's cheaper and often better quality. Make the pieces more or less the same size so that they will cook evenly, and add the dark meat to the pan first because it takes longer to cook. When it is done, drain the chicken on paper towels. Place the pieces over rice in a large heated dish and spoon the Black Bean Sauce* over them (the sauce should be prepared ahead of time). Chop scallion tops and scatter over the dish for decoration.

FRIED BEAN SPROUTS

2 cans (5 oz.) bean sprouts
3 tblsp. vegetable or peanut oil
2 slices ginger, chopped (or 1 tsp. powdered)

4 scallions
2 tblsp. soy sauce
Salt and pepper

Drain bean sprouts. Heat oil in skillet. Add ginger. Chop scallions and add to skillet. Stir-fry for 1 minute. Add bean sprouts and cook for 2 minutes. Add soy sauce and seasoning and cook for 2 minutes. Serves 4.

DUK (PLUM) SAUCE*
SWEET AND SOUR MUSTARD GREENS

Sautéed Chicken
Rice

To go with the chicken we suggest rice and Sweet and Sour Mustard Greens to which we have added 8 baby tomatoes as an option. Remember that color is one of the basic features of Chinese cooking. Serve the chicken over the rice.

You can use either bottled Duk Sauce* to dip the chicken or make it yourself ahead of time using the simple recipe we have listed in the Index.

SWEET AND SOUR MUSTARD GREENS

1 lb. mustard greens
4 tblsp. peanut or vegetable oil
8 baby tomatoes (optional)
Salt and pepper
2 tblsp. sugar

2 tblsp. soy sauce
2 tblsp. vinegar
2 tblsp. cornstarch mixed with
2 tblsp. dry sherry

Cut up greens into large pieces. Heat oil in skillet. Stir-fry greens until tender. If baby tomatoes are used, stir-fry along with the greens. Season, add sugar, soy sauce, vinegar, and cornstarch-sherry mixture. Stir until mixture coats the spoon. Serves 4.

DUCK

Duck is the favorite Chinese dish. One of the great things about cooking it in the Chinese style is that this eliminates most of the fat. This is about the only meat the Chinese cook whole. They cut it up into small pieces after they have cooked it.

Most of the duck you will find in the supermarket is frozen, but this does not have the devastating effect that it has on chicken. Thaw it out in the refrigerator for a day, or place it in a basin and run it under a cold tap. Never thaw it with hot water.

To prepare it remove all the loose fat and yellow bits around the cavity. Cut off the fat glands from the tail. Puncture the skin along the back and thighs to allow some of the fat to escape while cooking.

There's much less meat on a duck than on a chicken, but the carcass will make great soup and stocks afterward. If you're cooking for two, buy a larger duck and save half to eat cold.

Don't overcook duck or it will become very dry. It is done when the juices run a pale rosy yellow.

To get a good crisp skin on duck, brown it on all sides (in its own fat) before you put it in the oven.

CHINESE DUCK WITH BLACK BEAN SAUCE*

Peas

This is a recipe for roast duck with a Chinese overtone. We baste the duck with the marinating liquid and pour over a separately made Black Bean Sauce* at the end. Make the sauce while the duck is cooking.

We suggest that you roast some turnips, cut into small portions, or some peeled white radishes and onions with the duck. As far as any other vegetable is concerned we chose peas since they are light and sweet.

CHINESE DUCK WITH BLACK BEAN SAUCE*

1 duck (4-5 lbs.)

Marinade

2 tblsp. dry sherry
1 tsp. ginger powder
1 tsp. soy sauce
1 tsp. cornstarch mixed
    with 1 tsp. water

1 tsp. water
Salt and pepper
1½ c. Black Bean Sauce*

Preheat oven to 350° F. Cut all fatty tissues away from duck and dry thoroughly. In bowl mix sherry, ginger powder, soy sauce, cornstarch, and seasoning. Leave duck in marinade for at least half an hour. Roast in oven for 1½-2 hours, basting. Serve sauce in separate dish. Serves 4.

ORANGE DUCK

Brown Rice

Since orange duck is such a great American favorite it was essential to include a recipe for it cooked in a Chinese style. The duck is stuffed with a combination of Chinese and American ingredients and roasted on a rack over water (this helps to get rid of the fat).

We've added a touch of our own for the stuffing: baby food pears. This gives a sweet-sour flavor against the soy sauce.

Brown rice is one of the most delicious companions to this dish. If you are having a green vegetable, a green unsweet one cooked in the Chinese way would be an excellent accompaniment.

ORANGE DUCK

1 duck (4-5 lbs.)

Stuffing

Duck liver
1 onion
1 clove garlic
3 slices fresh ginger (or 1 tsp. powdered)
1 tblsp. peanut or vegetable oil
½ c. soy sauce

2 tblsp. dry sherry
1 tsp. brown sugar
2 orange peels, finely minced
1 jar (4½ oz.) baby food pears (optional)
Salt and pepper

Preheat oven to 350° F. Wash duck, remove all fatty tissue, and dry thoroughly, including cavity. Mince duck liver, onion, garlic, and ginger. Heat oil in skillet. Stir-fry minced ingredients for 2 minutes. Place in bowl. To bowl add soy sauce, sherry, sugar, orange peel, and pears, if desired. Season. Stuff cavity and sew up. Place on rack in drip pan over water and cook for about 1½ to 2 hours until the juices run pale rosy yellow. Serves 4.

ROAST MARINATED DUCK

Roast Potatoes
Green Vegetable

The duck is cooked in the traditional way but it is first marinated, then cooked, in a Chinese sauce. Cook the potatoes in the same pan with the duck.

Be sure to remove all the fatty glands from the

bird and puncture the skin so that the marinade mixture will penetrate. If you're cooking this dish for two, buy a larger duck and serve it cold on another day.

ROAST MARINATED DUCK

1 duck (about 4-5 lbs.)	3 tblsp. sherry
2 cloves garlic	Salt and pepper
3 scallions	2 tblsp. brown sugar
3 tblsp. soy sauce	

Preheat oven to 350° F. Wash duck, remove fatty glands, and wipe dry. Mince garlic and scallions. Place in bowl and add soy sauce, sherry, and seasoning. Put duck in bowl and work mixture well into the skin. Leave to stand for half an hour.

Cover skin with brown sugar. Place in roasting pan, surrounded by potatoes. Pour half marinade mixture over it and pour the rest inside the cavity. Roast for about 1¾ to 2 hours, until the juices run a pale rosy yellow. Baste every 15 minutes, turning the potatoes so that they are done on all sides. Serves 4.

STEAMED DUCK

Potatoes on Rice
  Green Vegetable

The traditional Chinese way with duck is to steam it. This method eliminates all the fat. After it is steamed you then fry it in oil to give it a good crisp skin.

Use a Long Island duckling, puncture the skin all over with a fork, and let it stand for at least half an hour to let the marinade mixture soak in.

On the table serve Duk (Plum) Sauce*, Chinese Hot Mustard*, and soy sauce in little dishes.

Any traditional vegetable will go with the duck. If you want to be exotic you can use wild rice.

STEAMED DUCK

1 duck (4-5 lbs.)

Marinade

4 tblsp. dry sherry	1 tsp. Tabasco sauce
2 tsp. sugar	Salt and pepper
½ tsp. chili powder	4 tblsp. flour
4 slices ginger, chopped	2 eggs, beaten
(or 1 tsp. powdered)	3 c. vegetable or peanut oil
1 tsp. anise powder	

Wash duck, remove all fatty tissue, dry thoroughly on paper towels, puncture skin with fork. In bowl mix sherry, sugar, chili powder, ginger, anise, Tabasco, and seasoning. Let duck stand basted in mixture for at least half an hour. Cover in steamer and steam for 1½ hours. Remove duck and cool.

Mix flour, eggs, and seasoning. Coat duck with the mixture. In deep skillet heat oil. Deep-fry duck until skin is brown and crispy. Serves 4.

BEEF

The Chinese do not eat nearly as much meat as Westerners do. Cattle were valued as beasts of burden and seldom eaten. When it was eaten, meat was never served in large chunks the way it is in America. The Chinese always chopped it and cooked it with vegetables so that the flavors would complement each other.

The flesh should be red and marbled with little veins of fat. The fat should be cream-colored. Learn to notice the difference between meat that has been thawed and fresh meat. Thawed meat has a damp, sodden look to it.

When you stir-fry beef, never cook it for longer

than 2 minutes or so before you add the vegetables or it will toughen.

Flank steak is one of the best cuts for stir-frying. It should be sliced paper thin against the grain. You will find this is one of the cheaper cuts too.

When you're buying ground meat, choose a cut and have the butcher grind it in front of you. This way you can be sure of getting good quality.

FRIED BAMBOO SHOOTS WITH MUSTARD GREENS

Beef and Onion Stew

Since beef and onion stew is a fairly heavy dish you need no other vegetables besides the bamboo shoots and mustard greens. However you may want to include potatoes in the stew.

The mustard greens *must* be dry before they are fried. Either dry them on paper towels or twirl them in a salad shaker. The same applies to the bamboo shoots.

FRIED BAMBOO SHOOTS WITH MUSTARD GREENS

1 can (5 oz.) bamboo shoots, drained
1 lb. fresh mustard greens (leaves only)
1 hot pepper
1 c. peanut or vegetable oil
Salt and pepper

Drain and dry bamboo shoots and mustard greens. Dice hot pepper. In skillet heat oil. Add bamboo shoots, fry until brown and remove from pan to drain on paper towels. Add mustard greens and pepper. Fry for 2 minutes or until tender. Remove to heated dish with bamboo shoots. Season and serve. Serves 4.

BRAISED CURRIED BEEF

Avocado Salad
Rice

This is an unusual combination bringing Chinese, American, and Indian elements to the same dish. It is excellent either for a winter dinner or a buffet lunch. Serve it with beer.

For decoration slice some hard-boiled eggs, sprinkle them with red paprika, and place them over the beef dish.

You can add flavor to the avocado salad by dropping an egg yolk and a teaspoonful of the braised beef sauce into the mayonnaise.

BRAISED CURRIED BEEF

2 lbs. stewing beef, cut into 1″ cubes
1 c. vegetable or peanut oil
2 onions, chopped
3 tblsp. curry powder (or more or less depending on how strong you wish it)
1 tsp. cumin

4 slices ginger, chopped (or 1 tsp. powdered)
1 tsp. sugar
2 c. heated chicken stock
2 tblsp. cornstarch mixed with
3 tblsp. water
Salt and pepper

Remove filaments from beef cubes and dry meat on paper towels. Heat oil in skillet. Brown beef quickly on all sides over high heat. Remove and drain on paper towels. Turn down heat and add onions. Cook until clear; do not burn. Add curry powder and cumin. Cook for 2 minutes. Add ginger, sugar, and heated stock. Return meat to pan, cover and cook for about 1-1½ hours, or until meat is tender. Add blended cornstarch and water; bring to boil until sauce coats spoon. Serve on bed of rice and decorate with eggs and paprika if desired. Serves 4-6.

CUBED STEWING BEEF WITH BLACK BEAN SAUCE*

Rice
Broccoli or Spinach

Chuck stewing steak is usually pretty tough and has to be cooked for quite a while before it becomes tender. In this recipe it's cooked for only a couple of minutes, so it remains slightly rare inside, keeps all its juices, and doesn't get tough. The sauce is made after the meat is cooked. Meanwhile you can have whatever other vegetables you choose cooked the American way. We suggest rice, or even mashed potatoes, and a green vegetable.

CUBED STEWING BEEF WITH BLACK BEAN SAUCE*

2 lbs. chuck stewing beef   3 c. Black Bean Sauce*
3 tblsp. peanut or vegetable oil

Chop the stewing beef into 1-inch cubes and remove all fatty filament. Heat skillet; add oil. When sizzling, add beef. Sear rapidly on all sides and remove to a heated dish. In skillet make Black Bean Sauce*. You will notice blood on the dish where the meat is being kept warm. Add this to the sauce with the meat to keep warm while you serve up the rice and vegetable. Serves 4-6.

FRIED BEEF WITH CAULIFLOWER

Potatoes
Salad

The cauliflower has to be parboiled for 3 minutes

138

before it is fried in the pan since it is a tough vegetable and won't become tender through mere frying. While you prepare the cauliflower, marinate the beef in the ginger and soy sauce mixture.

FRIED BEEF WITH CAULIFLOWER

2 lbs. stewing beef, sliced thinly	½ pkg. (10 oz.) frozen snow peas, thawed
1 tsp. ginger powder	1 parboiled cauliflower (broken into flowerets)
2 tblsp. soy sauce	
2 egg whites	2 tblsp. dry sherry
2 tblsp. cornstarch	Salt and pepper
2 c. peanut or vegetable oil	

Marinate the beef slices in ginger powder and soy sauce. Dry. Combine egg whites with cornstarch and coat the beef slices with the mixture. Heat oil in skillet. Fry beef for 3 minutes or until tender. Remove and drain on paper towels. Pour out two-thirds of oil from skillet. Heat rest and add snow peas and cooked cauliflower (remember to drain it first). Cook for 2 minutes. Add sherry and seasoning. Return beef to pan. Cook 2 minutes and serve. Serves 4.

FRIED BEEF WITH SNOW PEAS

Potatoes Au Gratin

This is a very good way to cook the cheaper cuts of beef since it assures their tenderness.

We suggest potatoes au gratin since they can be sliced and cooked in the oven with milk and cheese while you attend to the chopping and cutting of the Chinese dish. Don't cook the beef until the potatoes are done. Keep them warm in the oven while you prepare it.

FRIED BEEF WITH SNOW PEAS

2 lbs. stewing beef, sliced and cut into small cubes
1 tsp. sherry
3 tblsp. soy sauce
1 tsp. flour
½ c. peanut or vegetable oil

1 pkg. (10 oz.) frozen snow peas, thawed
1 clove garlic, crushed
½ tsp. onion powder
½ c. chicken broth
Salt and pepper

Marinate beef in sherry, soy sauce, and flour for at least 20 minutes. Heat two-thirds oil in skillet. Add beef and stir-fry for 3 minutes or until tender. Remove to drain on paper towels. Heat rest of oil in skillet. Add snow peas and crushed garlic. Cook for 2 minutes. Add beef to pan plus onion powder, broth, and seasoning. Cook for 1 more minute. Serve immediately. Serves 4.

GREEN BEANS WITH BAMBOO SHOOTS FRIED NOODLES

Roast Beef

Before you put the beef in the oven, coat it with Chinese Hot Mustard* mixed with a little soy sauce or beer. Use yesterday's noodles by frying them in peanut or vegetable oil with any kind of chopped leftover meat or vegetable. Green Beans with Bamboo Shoots go well and they are quick and easy.

GREEN BEANS WITH BAMBOO SHOOTS

1 lb. fresh or 1 pkg. (10 oz.) frozen beans
3 tblsp. peanut or vegetable oil
1 can (5 oz.) bamboo shoots, drained

¼ tsp. sugar
Salt and pepper
¾ c. water

140

If fresh beans are used, slice into 2 inch pieces; if using frozen ones, thaw and dry. Heat oil in skillet. Add beans and cook for 5 minutes over high heat, stirring constantly. Add bamboo shoots, sugar, salt and pepper. Stir. Add water. Cook over low heat for 7 minutes. Correct seasoning and drain any remaining liquid. Serves 4.

FRIED NOODLES

½ lb. cold, cooked noodles
3 tblsp. peanut or vegetable oil
Salt and pepper
Leftover chopped ham, mushrooms, shrimp, pork, etc. (optional)

1 tsp. cornstarch mixed with
1 tsp. water
3 tblsp. soy sauce
½ c. hot water

Fry noodles in heated oil for 3 minutes. Season. Add optional leftovers. Stir in cornstarch mixture, soy sauce, and hot water. Cook 3 minutes or until sauce thickens. Serves 4.

FRIED CABBAGE WITH MUSHROOMS

London Broil
Rice or Potatoes

This simple London broil dish is greatly improved by the addition of Chinese vegetables. You can also make it more interesting by placing some little dishes of Chinese condiments, soy sauce, Chinese Hot Mustard*, and Oyster Sauce*, on the table.

Don't fry the cabbage until the meat is done. It is better to parboil the sections before you fry them since the mushrooms cook very much quicker.

Serve the dish with potatoes or rice. For color effect, cook 8 baby tomatoes with the cabbage.

141

FRIED CABBAGE WITH MUSHROOMS

¾ lb. fresh mushrooms	1 tsp. sugar
1 medium-sized green cabbage	2 tsp. sherry
6 tblsp. peanut or vegetable oil	Salt and pepper

Slice mushrooms and soak for half an hour in salted water. Drain. Cut cabbage into 2 inch cubes and parboil. Drain. Heat oil in skillet. Add cabbage and stir-fry for 1 minute. Add mushrooms and cook until tender. Add sugar and sherry. Broil for 2 minutes. Season and serve. Serves 4-6.

OYSTER SAUCE*
BRAISED TURNIPS

Meat Loaf
Rice (Optional)

Here's a way to make a meat and potatoes dinner into something different. Instead of potatoes, try Chinese Braised Turnips. Serve the meat with Oyster Sauce* and perhaps a bowl of rice on the side.

Put a few pimiento-stuffed olives into the meat loaf mixture before you cook it. When it's sliced you'll have a pretty mosaic pattern. You could even add halved mushrooms or chopped cucumber.

Timing is the secret of success here. While the meat loaf is cooking, make your sauce. And during the last 15 minutes do the turnips so they'll be ready just as you take your meat loaf out of the oven. Remember that cold meat loaf is delicious, so if you're planning a buffet or luncheon later, save it to go with one of our Chinese salads.

BRAISED TURNIPS

3 tblsp. peanut or vegetable oil
6 small white turnips,
  coarsely grated or
  sliced very thin
Salt

¾ c. water
2 small onions, grated or
  diced
1½ tblsp. soy sauce
Pepper

Heat oil in heavy skillet. Sauté turnips for 1 minute, stirring constantly. Add salt and water. Cover and cook over low heat for 5 minutes. Stir in onions, soy sauce, and pepper. Cook for 5 minutes. Remove mixture to a warm dish. Cover, serve.

Note: *If onions are diced, not grated, cook them first until clear. This recipe can be combined with mashed potatoes if turnips and onions are grated.*

ASPARAGUS IN GINGER SHERRY SAUCE

Pan-Broiled Steak
  Potatoes or Rice

This is a very good combination and a different way of cooking asparagus when it is in season. Here the asparagus is blanched before it is added to the skillet.

Pan-broiled steak is often much more tender than grilled steak because the hot pan seals in the juices. Remember to dry the meat thoroughly before you add it to the pan otherwise it won't brown.

ASPARAGUS IN GINGER SHERRY SAUCE

1 lb. fresh asparagus
  spears
1 tblsp. peanut or vegetable oil

2 slices ginger, chopped
  (or 1 tsp. ground)
3 tblsp. dry sherry
Salt and pepper

143

Dice asparagus into ½ inch pieces. Drop all except tips into boiling salted water for 3 minutes. Drain and place on heated dish. Heat oil in skillet. Add ginger. Stir-fry for 1 minute, add asparagus and stir-fry 2 minutes. Add sherry, bring to boil, season and serve. Serves 4.

FRIED BAMBOO SHOOTS WITH CHILI SAUCE CHINESE HOT MUSTARD*

Salisbury Steak

This vegetable dish goes very well with beef. We suggest here that you spoon it over the meat when you serve it. It makes a quick economical meal.

Use good ground meat for the Salisbury steak. There's nothing worse than greasy, fatty hamburger. Put a little Chinese Hot Mustard* and some finely chopped scallion tops in the meat mixture.

FRIED BAMBOO SHOOTS WITH CHILI SAUCE

2 cans (5 oz.) bamboo shoots	1 tblsp. soy sauce
1 chili pepper	1 tsp. sugar
1 c. vegetable or peanut oil	Salt and cayenne red pepper
2 tsp. chili sauce	

Drain and dry bamboo shoots. Dice chili pepper. In skillet heat oil. Fry bamboo shoots and pepper until golden. Remove and drain on paper towels. Discard oil, leaving 2 tablespoons in pan. Heat and add chili sauce, soy sauce, sugar. Add vegetables. Season. Cook for 2 minutes and serve. Serves 4.

MIXED VEGETABLES

Steak
  Rice
  or Potatoes

We suggest you marinate the steak first in a mixture of oil, garlic, and soy sauce to give it a Chinese flavor. You can then pour the vegetables over the steak when you serve it.

Use your imagination with the vegetables. You can substitute other kinds if you wish, or add leftovers to the pan toward the end of the cooking process. The tougher uncooked vegetables must be parboiled before they are added to the pan.

MIXED VEGETABLES

¼ cabbage
2 carrots
1 cucumber
1 stalk celery
½ can (5 oz.) bamboo shoots
¼ pkg. (10 oz.) frozen snow peas, thawed

5 tblsp. peanut or vegetable oil
½ c. chicken stock
1 tsp. sugar
2 tsp. soy sauce
Salt and pepper
½ tsp. chopped parsley (optional)

Cut cabbage into ½ inch cubes and parboil. Shred carrots. If you have a potato peeler shred them very fine and you won't need to parboil. Otherwise shred into 1½ inch strips. Peel and slice cucumber. Chop celery finely. Drain bamboo shoots and dry snow peas. In skillet heat oil. Add cabbage and stir-fry for 2 minutes. Add carrots and celery and cook for 1 minute. Add rest of vegetables and stir-fry for 2 minutes. Add stock, sugar, and soy sauce. Cover and simmer for 4 minutes. Season, sprinkle with parsley and serve. Serves 4.

CHINESE SALAD
· FRIED RICE

Steak

This is a good way to change a steak dinner into something quite different. Try marinating the steak in ½ cup soy sauce and ½ cup sherry before you cook it. While it's sitting, start your rice and salad. Prepare the salad first—don't add the dressing until you're just about to serve it. Refrigerate the cabbage so that it will be crisp. Start the rice. If you want your steak medium-rare, start cooking when you put the rice in the pan. If you want it very rare or well done, time accordingly.

CHINESE SALAD

    1 raw cabbage

Dressing

    2 tsp. leftover pickle juice   1 tsp. ground ginger
        (or 1 tsp. soy sauce, 1   2 tsp. soy sauce
        tsp. vinegar)   Salt and pepper
    2 tsp. vinegar

Shred cabbage finely, against the grain. Refrigerate. Combine all ingredients for dressing in bowl. Pour over cabbage at last minute and toss. Correct seasoning. Serves 4-6.

FRIED RICE

    ½ lb. smoked bacon in ¼"   4 c. cold cooked rice
        cubes   2 eggs, beaten
     1 small white onion,   2 tsp. soy sauce
        chopped   Salt and pepper

Fry bacon over medium-high heat. Stir in onion, turn down heat, and fry till soft. Add rice. Cook for 2 minutes. Stir in eggs, soy sauce, and seasoning. Cook for 1 minute.

NOTE: *You can add peppers, any vegetable, or meat. This is a good way to use leftovers.*

Fried Rice can be frozen and used again, so you might want to make a double supply.

STEAK AND ONIONS

String Beans
Mashed Potatoes

This method of cooking a traditional steak and onion dinner will make it taste completely unlike the usual one you know. You can also use less meat than you would use to cook it the American way.

Be sure that the pan is large enough to hold the meat so that it is evenly cooked. Before you cook it, prepare the string beans and potatoes. Keep them warm in the oven while you do the last-minute frying of the steak and onions. That will take only a couple of minutes—but remember, everything must be chopped ahead of time.

STEAK AND ONIONS

1 lb. rump steak
2 large yellow or Spanish onions
4 tblsp. peanut or vegetable oil
1 clove garlic, crushed
1 c. hot chicken bouillon or chicken stock

1 tblsp. sherry
1 tsp. soy sauce
1 tsp. cornstarch mixed with
1 tsp. cold water
Salt and pepper

Cut steak, against the grain, into very thin strips. Slice onions thinly. Heat skillet, add half the oil, and when hot add onions. Cook until golden. Remove from pan and wipe pan with paper towel. Heat remaining oil and add crushed garlic clove. Fry for 3 minutes, then discard and add the meat. Fry for 1 minute—no more or the meat will be tough and stringy. Remove and keep warm with onion in heated dish. Add hot stock, sherry, soy sauce, and cornstarch mixture to pan. Bring to boil for 2 minutes or until the sauce is thick enough to coat the spoon. Season and return the beef and onion to the pan. Toss around till covered with sauce. Serves 4.

STEAK AND OYSTER SAUCE*

Buttered Zucchini
  Potato Dumplings

This is a classical Chinese recipe and can be used for all kinds of steak. You can even cook the sauce separately and pour it over a whole steak.

Serve it with buttered zucchini—you can vary this by peeling the zucchini—it cooks faster—and potato dumplings cooked in chicken broth.

STEAK AND OYSTER SAUCE*

2 lbs. flank steak	1 tsp. soy sauce
1 c. peanut or vegetable oil	2 tsp. cornstarch mixed with
4 tblsp. Oyster Sauce*	2 tsp. sherry
1 tsp. sugar	Salt and pepper
1/2 c. chicken stock	

Slice meat thinly against the grain. Heat oil in skillet. Add meat and cook for 2 minutes until browned. Mix Oyster Sauce*, sugar, chicken stock, and soy sauce in bowl. Add to skillet. Cover and cook over medium heat for 2 minutes. Add cornstarch mixture, season, and cook until sauce coats spoon. Serves 4.

LAMB

Lamb is used in Northern China where the people are Moslems and do not eat pork. It is not, however, used much in other regions. The Chinese use mutton more than we use it; most of the cuts you'll find in the supermarket are young.

Lamb can be twice as good if it is marinated for a few days in the refrigerator before it is cooked. Yoghurt ensures a crisp flesh and a soft inside; a spread of mustard, oil, and herbs also makes a good marinade.

When you prepare a leg of lamb shave off the loose fat and ink markings. Choose very pale pink flesh. The smaller cuts of lamb are younger. The darker, larger ones are tougher and less sweet.

MIXED VEGETABLES
FRIED RICE*

Lamb Chops

Turn the chops in a mixture of 1 tablespoon mustard, 2 tablespoons soy sauce, and 2 tablespoons oil with ¼ teaspoon thyme or rosemary. Let them stand in the mixture for at least half an hour.

Meanwhile, chop the vegetables and add them to the skillet when the chops are nearly done. The recipe calls for parboiling before frying. This is so that the tougher vegetables won't be undercooked.

Since we don't usually mix vegetables together in the way that the Chinese do, this may seem an unusual combination to many Americans. However you should use your imagination and add other varieties of vegetables or leftovers.

Turn to the Index to locate the Fried Rice* recipe and prepare after that the mixed vegetables, keeping them warm in the oven meanwhile.

MIXED VEGETABLES

¼ lb. string beans	½ c. peanut or vegetable oil
¼ lb. broccoli	½ tsp. salt
¼ lb. small white mushrooms	½ c. chicken stock
1 onion	Pepper
1 clove garlic	

Cut string beans into sections 1 inch long. Divide broccoli into flowerets. Parboil. Slice mushrooms, onions, and crush garlic clove. In skillet heat oil. Add onion and garlic. Salt and stir-fry for 1 minute. Add string beans and broccoli. Stir-fry for 1 minute. Add mushrooms and stir-fry for 1 minute. Pour in stock, bring to rapid boil, and cook for 3 minutes. Season and serve. Serves 4.

LAMB AND MUSHROOMS

Buttered Noodles
Watercress Salad

The lamb is sliced quite differently from any American way. It is cut paper-thin against the grain, almost as one would slice veal, so that it cooks quickly. It is then simmered with vegetables until the sauce thickens enough to coat the spoon.

Serve it with large flat buttered noodles. These can be three-quarters cooked ahead of time, rinsed, drained, and refrigerated. When you are ready to use them drop them into boiling water for 1 minute and drain.

Other vegetables are not really necessary since there are plenty with the lamb. However a watercress salad would go very well. Make a simple dressing of 1 tablespoon lemon juice, 1 crushed clove garlic, and 3 tablespoons oil.

LAMB AND MUSHROOMS

2 lbs. stewing lamb	1 c. chicken stock
3 tblsp. peanut or vegetable oil	1 tblsp. cornstarch
4 slices ginger, chopped	1 tsp. dry sherry
½ tsp. salt	2 tsp. soy sauce
1 lb. sliced fresh mushrooms	1 squeeze lemon (optional)
1 can (5 oz.) bamboo shoots	2 tsp. chopped parsley (optional)
	Pepper

Cut lamb into cubes and slice paper thin against the grain. In skillet heat oil. Add ginger and salt. Sauté for 1 minute. Add sliced mushrooms, drained bamboo shoots. Sauté for 5 minutes, stirring constantly. Add lamb and sauté for 5 minutes. Heat stock and pour in. Cover and simmer until stock has reduced by half. In bowl blend cornstarch with sherry and soy sauce. Add to skillet. Bring to boil and cook until sauce coats spoon. If desired, add squeeze of lemon and chopped parsley. Season and serve. Serves 4-6.

FRAGRANT STEWED LAMB CHOPS

New Potatoes
Green Vegetable

Get your butcher to cut for you the required amount of shoulder lamb chops. Marinate them overnight. They are then dried and browned, seasoned, and stewed in the marinade mixture and chicken stock for about 2 hours.

The heat must be very high when you brown the lamb, and for the scallions and ginger. Keep stirring constantly. If you stop for a minute the food will burn.

You can add a small cubed turnip to the stew. It will absorb the flavor of the stew and make an interesting addition. Apart from that, new potatoes and a green vegetable such as broccoli, cabbage, or peas would be the best accompaniments.

FRAGRANT STEWED LAMB CHOPS

8 shoulder lamb chops	2 cloves garlic, crushed
1 c. soy sauce	4 scallions, chopped
2 tblsp. dry sherry	3 slices ginger, chopped
2 tblsp. brown sugar	3 cloves
½ tsp. ginger powder	½ tsp. anise powder
1 tsp. salt	½ tsp. curry powder
Pepper	½ tsp. chopped mint
4 tblsp. peanut or vegetable oil	3 c. chicken stock

Trim chops. In large bowl mix soy sauce, sherry, brown sugar, ginger powder, and seasoning. Marinate chops in mixture overnight or for at least an hour. In skillet heat oil. Dry chops, reserving marinade, and sauté lightly until browned. Remove to plate. Add garlic, scallions, and ginger. Stir-fry for 1 minute. Add cloves, anise powder, curry powder, and mint. Stir-fry for 30 seconds. Meanwhile heat stock and add to pan. Bring to boil. Add marinade mixture and chops. Cover and simmer for 2 hours or until the chops are tender. Serves 4-6.

MARINADE
SWEET AND SOUR MUSTARD GREENS*

Grilled Lamb Chops
Baked Potatoes

The secret here is the marinade and this is guaranteed to improve any chop. Marinate them for at least an hour but preferably overnight.

If you want to get the charcoal grilled effect without a charcoal grill, you can achieve this by drying the chops, sprinkling them with charcoal powder and lemon juice. Wrap them in foil paper and bake them in a moderate (350° F.) oven for twenty minutes. Then open the paper and let them cook for 10 minutes more so that they become crisp on the outside.

Bake the potatoes at the same time that you cook the chops. Turn to the Index for the Sweet and Sour Mustard Greens* recipe. If you prefer, a watercress salad would go equally well with this dish too.

MARINADE

½ c. soy sauce	2 cloves garlic, crushed
1 tsp. sesame oil (or peanut oil if not available)	2 scallions, chopped
½ c. sherry	Salt and pepper

Mix all ingredients in bowl. Marinate chops in mixture. Serves 4, allowing 8 chops, 2 per person.

DUK (PLUM) SAUCE*
BRAISED ENDIVE

Roast Lamb
Roast Potatoes

Before you roast the lamb let it set in a mixture of 1 cup yoghurt, 2 tablespoons soy sauce, and 3 chopped cloves garlic for a day or so (for a 5 pound lamb) in the refrigerator. The flesh will be tender and full of flavor and the outside will be crisp. Roast the potatoes in the oven with the lamb.

We suggest a Chinese way of braising endive and a dish of Duk Sauce* as a different combination with the roast lamb.

When you buy endive look for the fresher, whiter ones. They are usually sold in a box, so pick out the ones underneath that have not been spoiled by exposure.

BRAISED ENDIVE

6 Chinese dried mushrooms, soaked in water overnight (or for 30 min.)	3 tblsp. soy sauce
	¼ c. chicken broth
	1 tsp. sugar
6 endive	1 tblsp. dry sherry
4 tblsp. peanut or vegetable oil	Salt and pepper

Drain and slice the soaked mushrooms. Slice the endive. In skillet heat oil. Add mushrooms and endive. Cook over medium heat for 5 minutes. Add soy sauce, broth, sugar, and sherry. Cover and cook 15 minutes. Season and serve. Serves 6.

STUFFING
SAUTEED EGGPLANT

Roast Lamb
Rice

Buy a 5 pound lamb and get your butcher to bone it. Wash it out and dry thoroughly. Smear a little oil on the inside. Fill with stuffing and tie up for roasting. Cook for the same time that you would a roast lamb with bone in.

Rice would go well with this dish. The Sautéed Eggplant is also an excellent accompaniment for lamb. Don't start cooking it until the lamb is ready. Chop the eggplant into cubes before you put the lamb into the oven. Dry and let them stand salted with kosher salt until you are ready to cook them—at least for an hour.

STUFFING

1 tsp. peanut or vegetable oil
1 clove garlic, mashed
2 tblsp. chopped scallions
2 slices fresh ginger, chopped (or ½ tsp. powdered)
1 tsp. salt
1 tsp. fresh chopped parsley
½ tsp. rosemary
1 tsp. finely chopped Chinese dried mushrooms, soaked in water overnight (or for 30 min.)
1 tsp. soy sauce
½ c. cooked rice
Pepper

In skillet heat oil. Fry garlic, scallions, and ginger. Salt and remove to mixing bowl. To bowl add parsley, rosemary, drained mushrooms, and soy sauce. Add rice and season. Mix together and stuff lamb. Makes about 1 cup stuffing.

SAUTÉED EGGPLANT

2 lbs. eggplant
Salt
1 clove garlic
3 large Chinese dried mushrooms, soaked in water overnight (or for 30 min.)
3 tblsp. peanut or vegetable oil
2 tblsp. soy sauce
1 c. chicken broth
Pepper

Peel and slice eggplant, salt, and let stand for an hour. Chop garlic and mushrooms (drained). In skillet heat oil. Add garlic and fry until golden. Add mushrooms, stir-fry for 1 minute. Dry eggplant and brown on all sides. Add soy sauce, broth, and seasoning. Bring to boil. Cover and simmer for abut 20-25 minutes. Serves 6.

LAMB STEW WITH BEAN SPROUTS AND PEAS

Rice
Salad

This is a "red" Chinese stew, meaning that it has soy sauce added. This flavoring is used for the stronger meats (as opposed to chicken or fish) and produces a good dark stew. The lamb cubes are fried in very hot oil to seal in their juices and then simmered on the stove for about 2 hours, or until the lamb is tender.

To peel the baby onions more easily, drop them into boiling water for 2 minutes. Drain and remove their skins at once.

Serve with rice and a salad.

LAMB STEW WITH BEAN SPROUTS AND PEAS

3 lbs. stewing lamb
3 tblsp. peanut or vegetable oil
2 cloves garlic, crushed
1 tsp. sugar
3 tblsp. flour
Salt and pepper
8 small white onions, peeled
3 cups chicken broth
2 tblsp. soy sauce
½ tsp. thyme or rosemary
1 bay leaf
1 can (5 oz.) bean sprouts
½ pkg. (10 oz.) frozen peas (thawed)

Cut the lamb into cubes about 1 inch square. In large pot heat oil. Add crushed garlic and lamb. Brown lamb on all sides quickly to sear in juices. Remove and sprinkle with sugar, flour, and seasoning. Discard oil in pot. Return lamb and garlic. Add onions, chicken broth, soy sauce, and herbs. Bring to boil. Turn down heat and cover. After an hour and a half of simmering add the bean sprouts and peas. Correct seasoning and serve. Serves 4-6.

RED STEWED LAMB

Baked Potatoes
Okra

We have combined Chinese and American methods of stewing in this recipe. The Chinese don't use an oven and do all their stewing on top of the stove. However this meal could be most easily prepared if you have the kind of casserole that can be used on top of the stove and in the oven. The frying is done on top and the stew is simmered in the oven. Make sure your casserole has a tight lid. This will ensure that none of the flavor escapes from the stew.

Bake the potatoes. Okra is one of the best vegetables as far as lamb is concerned. Serve it buttered; either fresh or frozen will do and prepare while lamb is cooking.

RED STEWED LAMB

2 tblsp. peanut or vegetable oil
3 lbs. stewing lamb, chopped into 1″ cubes
1 onion, chopped into large hunks
4 slices ginger, chopped (or 1 tsp. powdered)
3 stalks celery, chopped
½ tsp. salt
½ c. soy sauce
1 c. chicken stock
1 tsp. Tabasco sauce
Pepper

Preheat oven to 375° F. In casserole heat oil. Toss in lamb and brown. Remove to side dish. Lower heat. Add onion, ginger, celery, and salt. Fry until onion is clear. Remove onion mixture and discard oil. Return lamb and onion mixture to casserole. Add soy sauce, stock, Tabasco, and seasoning. Bring to boil and simmer for 10 minutes. Remove from stove and bake, covered, in oven for 3 hours. Serves 4-6.

Note: *If you do not have an ovenproof casserole, simmer the stew on top of the stove.*

STEWED LAMB
SAUTEED ESCAROLE

Potatoes or Rice

This lamb stew is cooked in a Western fashion using Chinese condiments. To decorate, scatter a little chopped parsley over the stew at the end.

Boil the chestnuts for about ½ hour and peel them while they are hot.

When the stew is done (and not before) prepare the escarole. After it is washed make sure that the leaves are dry (either use a salad twirler or dry on paper towels).

STEWED LAMB

2 lbs. lamb breast	¼ lb. mushrooms, sliced
3 tblsp. peanut or vegetable oil	¼ cup soy sauce
1 clove garlic, chopped	1 tsp. sugar
6 scallions	2 c. chicken stock
¼ lb. chestnuts, boiled and peeled	Salt and pepper

Chop lamb into 1 inch cubes. In skillet heat oil. Add garlic. Brown lightly. Add lamb piece by piece and brown on all sides. Remove and drain on paper towels. Chop scallions and fry until golden. Remove and drain. Add chestnuts and mushrooms. Stir-fry for half a minute. Add soy sauce, sugar, chicken stock, and seasoning. Return meat and scallions to skillet. Simmer for 2 hours or until meat is tender. Serves 4.

SAUTÉED ESCAROLE

1 lb. escarole leaves	1 tsp. sugar
2 tblsp. peanut or vegetable oil	Salt and pepper

Wash escarole and dry thoroughly. In skillet heat

oil. Add leaves and stir-fry for 5 minutes. Add sugar and seasoning. Serves 4.

LIVERS, KIDNEYS, AND HEARTS

Never buy frozen livers or kidneys. This meat must be completely fresh and should have no smell.

Liver should be cooked very fast over high heat so that the juices stay in and it does not become tough or curl up. Kidneys too should be cooked over very high heat, never for more than 2 or 3 minutes, so that the juices are not lost.

BEEF HEARTS WITH GINGER

Macaroni Au Gratin
String Beans in Butter

This is a hearty combination for a winter meal. Serve it with beer or a light red wine.

Buy medium-size beef hearts. They are tenderer than the large ones because they come from a younger animal. They must be fresh and with almost no smell. Marinating them for half an hour before they are cooked makes them much more tender.

Use the marinade for a sauce which will go well with the macaroni and cheese.

BEEF HEARTS WITH GINGER

2 beef hearts	½ tsp. salt
2 tsp. cornstarch	5 tblsp. peanut or vegetable oil
3 tblsp. dry sherry	
1 tblsp. soy sauce	3 scallions, chopped
1 tblsp. water	4 slices ginger, chopped
1 tsp. sugar	(or 1 tsp. powdered)

Trim off fat and blood vessels from hearts. Cut into

thin strips. In bowl mix cornstarch, sherry, soy sauce, water, sugar, and salt. Marinate hearts for half an hour.

Drain meat and reserve marinade. In pan heat oil. Add scallions and ginger. Fry for 2 minutes. Add hearts. Stir-fry for 3 minutes until done. Remove to heated dish. Add marinade to pan and boil. When the sauce coats the spoon, pour over meat and serve. Serves 4.

LIVER AND SCALLIONS

Rice
Squash

You can serve this dish over rice with almost any vegetable. Here we suggest squash sliced and cooked in water and butter. Its blandness would go well with the sharpness of the scallions.

You must cook the liver very fast over high heat so that it does not become tough. You must not overcook it. For this recipe you could cook the liver in a separate pan.

LIVER AND SCALLIONS

1 lb. liver	3 tblsp. soy sauce
Flour	1 tblsp. dry sherry
12 scallions	1 tsp. cornstarch mixed
5 tblsp. peanut or vegetable oil	with
	1 tsp. water
1 clove garlic, crushed	Salt and pepper
1 tsp. ginger powder	

Slice the liver into 1 inch cubes. Roll in flour. Mince scallions. Save green part to add to pan at end. In skillet heat oil. Add garlic and scallions (white part). Stir-fry for 3 minutes. Remove from pan. Add liver. Fry for 1 or 2 minutes. Remove to heated dish. Add ginger powder, soy sauce, and sherry. Bring to boil and add cornstarch mixture and seasoning. Add scallions, both white and green parts. Mix in liver and spoon over rice. Serve immediately. Serves 4.

MARINATED LIVER AND LEEKS

Noodles
Salad

This is a good dish for a luncheon party or dinner and can be made more interesting by the addition of any kind of green vegetable which you parboil and add at the end. Here we've chosen green peas.

Timing is essential to get this meal together. The liver must be chopped and marinated for half an hour before it is cooked. While it is marinating chop all the other ingredients. Then cook the noodles, and keep them warm. By this time you'll be ready for the frying and that whole operation takes only about 10 minutes.

Don't overcook the liver. Fry it lightly over very high heat for no more than 1 or 2 minutes or it will curl and toughen.

MARINATED LIVER AND LEEKS

1 pound liver	1 tsp. sugar
4 large white mushrooms	3 leeks
2 slices ginger, chopped (or 1 tsp. powdered)	2 scallions
	4 tblsp. peanut or vegetable oil
2 tblsp. dry sherry	
1 tblsp. soy sauce	1 clove garlic, crushed
2 tblsp. cornstarch blended with	½ tsp. Tabasco sauce
	½ c. parboiled peas (optional)
1 tblsp. water	

Cut away membranes from liver and slice thinly. Slice mushrooms. In bowl place ginger, sherry, soy sauce, blended cornstarch, and sugar. Leave liver and mushrooms to marinate for half an hour. Clean and chop leeks and scallions. Parboil leeks. In skillet heat oil. Fry crushed garlic for 1 minute. Add leeks and scallions and stir-fry for 3 minutes. Drain liver and mushroom mixture, reserving marinade, add to skillet, and stir-fry for 1 or 2 minutes. Add Tabasco, and peas if desired. Add marinade mixture and bring to boil. Turn over noodles and serve immediately. Serves 4.

VEAL KIDNEYS AND PEPPERS

Spaghetti

This gives an excellent Chinese touch to what is essentially an Italian meal. Serve the meat over spaghetti and drink a good red wine with it.

Prepare the spaghetti and keep warm. Don't fry the kidneys until the vegetables are done. Use two pans and fry the kidneys and vegetables separately. You must use a high heat, fry for no more than 1 or 2 minutes, and try not to lose the juices or the kidneys will become tough and tasteless. Serve at once or they will become hard.

VEAL KIDNEYS AND PEPPERS

1 lb. veal kidneys	1 clove garlic, crushed
2 green peppers	1 tsp. soy sauce
1 can (3 oz.) button mushrooms, drained	1 tsp. dry sherry
	½ c. chicken stock
1 can (5 oz.) water chestnuts, drained	1 tsp. cornstarch mixed with
½ c. peanut or vegetable oil	1 tsp. dry sherry
	Salt and pepper

Slice kidneys ¼ inch thick and remove any filament and tissue. Chop peppers, mushrooms, and water chestnuts into thin slices. Heat half the oil in skillet. Add crushed garlic. Cook until golden. Add peppers.

162

Cook for 1 minute. Add mushrooms and water chestnuts and cook for 1½ minutes. Add soy sauce, sherry, stock, and bring to boil. Add cornstarch-sherry mixture. Boil for about 2 minutes until mixture coats spoon. Season and turn into heated dish.

In another pan heat remainder of oil. Add the kidneys, season, and quick-fry for 1 minute over high heat. Spoon over vegetables and serve over spaghetti immediately. Serves 4.

FRIED SHREDDED VEAL LIVER WITH ONIONS AND CELERY

Peas
Mashed Potatoes

Liver and onions are always a good combination. Like the French, the Chinese have a great way of cooking it. We added celery to the dish for more flavor but you can omit it if you wish.

Leave the liver to stand for 15 minutes in the soy sauce and cornstarch while you prepare the other ingredients.

Peas and mashed potatoes are the traditional accompaniments with liver and they go very well in this case.

FRIED SHREDDED VEAL LIVER WITH ONIONS AND CELERY

1 lb. veal liver	2 stalks celery
2 tsp. cornstarch	1 c. peanut or vegetable oil
2 tblsp. soy sauce	Salt and pepper
3 onions	

Remove filament, cut up liver, and marinate in cornstarch and soy sauce. Chop onions and celery. In skillet heat oil. Fry onions until brown. Remove from skillet and drain on paper towels. Add celery and fry for 3 minutes. Remove and drain. Turn heat up and stir-fry liver for 1-2 minutes. Return onions and celery to pan. Mix together, season, and pour mixture over mashed potatoes. Serve at once. Serves 4.

PORK

Pork is a favorite meat of the Chinese. They cut it very finely and often cook it twice, removing the meat from the pan while the vegetables are cooking and adding it again at the end to ensure that it is fully cooked.

The raw flesh should be a pale-pink color, with a fair proportion of white fat. The meat should be firm to the touch. It tastes better and has more flavor cold if it is marinated before cooking. The meat should be thoroughly cooked without becoming overdone and dry. When done it has a white color.

BRAISED CURRIED PORK
WITH SWEET POTATOES
STRING BEANS AND BAMBOO SHOOTS*

This type of spicy Chinese cooking predominates in the Szechwan province in China where the climate is hot and almost tropical. The sweet potatoes used in this recipe contrast very well with the hot curry flavor.

You can cut short the cooking time of the potatoes by using canned ones. You won't have to deep-fry them, you can simply slice them and sauté them in a little oil.

Get your butcher to cut a pork shoulder into ½ inch cubes for you. The pieces should be small so that you can be sure that the meat is thoroughly cooked.

See Index to locate String Beans and Bamboo Shoots*. This is very simple and can be cooked at the last minute.

164

BRAISED CURRIED PORK WITH SWEET POTATOES

1 lb. pork, cut into ½″ cubes	4 slices fresh ginger, chopped (if available)
1 lb. sweet potatoes (or 1 can (1 lb.) drained	1 red-hot pepper, crushed
1 large white onion	3 tblsp. curry powder
3 c. peanut or vegetable oil for deep-frying	½ tsp. ginger powder
	2 tblsp. soy sauce
2 tblsp. peanut or vegetable oil for stir-frying	1 tblsp. dry sherry
	Salt and pepper
	1 c. chicken stock

Trim and cut pork if butcher has not already done so. Peel sweet potatoes and slice ½ inch thick. Shred onion. Heat deep-frying oil until smoking. Add sweet potatoes and deep-fry until golden. Remove and drain. In a skillet heat stir-frying oil. Add pork and brown on all sides. Remove to side dish. Add ginger, onion, crushed red pepper. Stir-fry for 1 minute. Add curry powder and ginger powder. Stir-fry for 1 minute. Return pork to pan. Add soy sauce, sherry, and seasoning. In another pan bring stock to boil and add to skillet. Add potatoes, cover skillet, and simmer over low heat for 40 minutes to an hour, until pork is done. Serves 4.

BAKED PORK WITH SALT CABBAGE (SAUERKRAUT)

Noodles

The Chinese rarely bake their foods since they do not have the fuel to do so. However, since baking is a favorite method of cooking in America, we have adapted this recipe for American cooking.

Salt cabbage is very hard to obtain so we have substituted sauerkraut. Noodles, either Chinese or Italian, would go well in this meal.

The sauerkraut is left to stand in sugar for 20 minutes and during that time the pork is left in a marinading mixture. They are then cooked together in the traditional Chinese way, except that we bake them instead of steaming. Use a baking dish that will go both on top of the stove and in the oven.

BAKED PORK WITH SALT CABBAGE (SAUERKRAUT)

½ lb. salt cabbage or sauerkraut
1 tblsp. sugar
1 lb. pork
1 tblsp. dry sherry
4 sices ginger, chopped (or 1 tsp. powdered)

1 tblsp. sesame oil (or peanut)
1 clove garlic, crushed
1 tblsp. soy sauce
Salt and pepper
1 tblsp. bacon fat
2 scallions

Drain and squeeze out the moisture from the sauerkraut. Mix sugar in and let it stand for 20 minutes. Slice pork into thin strips about 1½ inches long. In bowl mix together sherry, ginger, oil, garlic, soy sauce, and seasoning. Add pork and let stand for 20 minutes and dry before frying.

Preheat oven to 375° F. Heat baking dish over flame. Add bacon fat. When sizzling, add pork and sauerkraut. Cover with greaseproof paper and bake in oven for about half an hour or until cooked. Remove to serving dish. Chop scallions and sprinkle over. Serve at once. Serves 4.

FRIED PORK WITH SCALLIONS
FRIED ZUCCHINI*

Buttered Parsley
Potatoes

This pork recipe is very simple. It involves little chopping and takes only about 10 minutes to make.

Ask your butcher to shred the pork for you, or at

least to cut it into cubes so that it will be less trouble to shred. It must be shredded finely or it will be undercooked. Let the pork marinate for at least half an hour before you cook it.

You'll have to juggle with two pans here; the zucchini in one and the pork in the other. You can cut down the cooking time of the zucchini by peeling before you fry it. See Index to locate recipe.

To decorate the buttered potatoes sprinkle a little chopped parsley over them before they are served.

FRIED PORK WITH SCALLIONS

1 lb. pork	5 tblsp. peanut or vegeta-
2 tblsp. soy sauce	ble oil
1 tblsp. dry sherry	Salt
8 scallions	Pepper

Shred pork and mix in bowl with soy sauce and sherry. Marinate for half an hour. Chop scallions. In skillet heat oil. Dry pork and brown on all sides. Add scallions and salt. Stir-fry for 2 minutes. Cover and cook for 5-10 more minutes or until pork is done. Season and serve. Serves four.

DRY MARINADE
FRIED SWEET POTATOES
BEAN SPROUTS WITH GREEN PEPPERS*

Pork Chops

This combination is one of the most tasty sensations of Chinese cooking. You have the delicate sweetness of the potatoes combined with the subtle crunchy flavors of the bean sprouts and peppers. And pork chops make it a very inexpensive meal.

To save money, instead of buying individual chops,

buy a whole loin, cut off the amount you need, and freeze the rest for a roast later.

It's easier if you have two frying pans for the vegetables—then you can cook them at the same time during the last 15 minutes that the pork is cooking. If that's not possible, do the potatoes first. They'll keep warm in the sauce without overcooking. Check Index to locate Bean Sprouts with Green Peppers* recipe.

FRIED SWEET POTATOES

½ c. molasses	½ c. peanut or vegetable
¼ c. orange juice	oil
1 lb. sweet potatoes (or 1 can (1 lb.), drained)	Rock or kosher salt
	Pepper

Cook molasses over low heat for 10 minutes (do not boil). Add orange juice. While sauce is heating, peel and slice potatoes very thin. In a skillet heat oil and fry potatoes until they are golden brown. Dry on paper towles. Add salt (use rock or kosher salt) and pepper and arrange on heated platter. If the sauce is too thick (it should coat the spoon) add more orange juice and reheat. Season and pour over potatoes. Serves 4.

DRY MARINADE

Juice 1 lemon	Dash allspice
1 tsp. soy sauce	½ clove garlic, crushed
¼ tsp. ground sage or thyme	Salt and pepper

Mix ingredients together in bowl. Cover chops with the mixture and let stand at least an hour, overnight if possible.

MARINATED PORK CHOPS
SAUTEED ESCAROLE*

Noodles

The Chinese never cook meat whole (with the exception of duck, and even that is cut into little pieces for serving). Chops are no exception. They are usually boned (save the bones for stock) and cut into cubes before cooking.

Marinate the pork after you have chopped it so that the mixture will penetrate more areas. Let it stand in the mixture for at least half an hour.

Serve over noodles with Sautéed Escarole* (see Index).

MARINATED PORK CHOPS

6 thick pork chops	2 green peppers
4 slices ginger, chopped	1 tomato
1 clove garlic	1 tblsp. sugar
½ c. soy sauce	3 tblsp. peanut or vegetable oil
2 tblsp. dry sherry	ble oil
3 scallions	Salt and pepper

Bone the chops and cut the meat into 1 inch cubes. Place in mixing bowl. Add ginger, crushed garlic, 3 tablespoons of soy sauce, and sherry. Turn meat in mixture and let stand for half an hour.

Chop scallions and peppers. Skin tomato by dropping into scalding water. Chop. Combine the rest of the soy sauce with sugar. In skillet heat oil. Dry pork and brown on all sides. Add scallions, peppers, and tomato. Stir-fry for 3 minutes. Pour in soy sauce-sugar mixture. Stir-fry over high heat, bring to boil, cover, and simmer over low heat for about 20 minutes, or until pork is done. Season and serve. Serves 4.

SOY SAUCE MARINADE
CHINESE SAUCE
STIR-FRIED STRING BEANS AND ALMONDS

Roast Pork
Roast Potatoes

Pork can be roasted either in an open pan and basted frequently with a bulb baster or roasted in a covered casserole. The latter tenderizes the meat more and gets out the fat. Allow about 35-40 minutes per pound in a 325° F. oven.

We suggest you marinate the roast before you can cook it either overnight or for at least 6 hours. Save the marinade for possible use as a sauce for the pork.

To make the sauce, skim off the fat left in the bottom of the casserole or pan. You will be left with the cooking juices of the meat. There are many variations of sauces, Chinese style, using the juices and we suggest a couple here. One of the basic ingredients of the sauce is cornstarch, which thickens it to a good consistency. Be careful not to overcook or you'll be left with a sticky, gluey sauce.

SOY SAUCE MARINADE

1 c. soy sauce	2 tblsp. dry sherry
2 cloves garlic, crushed	Salt and pepper

Mix all ingredients together. Roll roast in the mixture until it is completely covered. Let it stand for at least 6 hours or overnight.

CHINESE SAUCE

½ c. cooking juices	3 tsp. soy sauce
2 tsp. cornstarch mixed with 2 tsp. water	2 tsp. dry sherry
	Salt and pepper

Scrape up coagulated cooking juices and bring to

170

boil. Add the cornstarch mixture. Boil for a few seconds. Add soy sauce and sherry. Season and boil until thick enough to coat spoon.

Note: *Never add sherry or any other wine or spirit to a sauce without boiling it. The alcohol gives off a harsh taste and you don't get the flavor.*

STIR-FRIED STRING BEANS AND ALMONDS

1 lb. string beans (or 1 pkg. (10 oz.) frozen)
2 tblsp. peanut or vegetable oil
3 slices ginger, chopped
1 c. blanched, peeled almonds

1 tblsp. soy sauce
½ tsp. sugar
¼ c. chicken stock
Salt and pepper

If beans are fresh parboil and dry before frying. If frozen, thaw and dry. In skillet heat oil. Add ginger and almonds and stir-fry for 1 minute. Add string beans and stir-fry for 1 minute. Add soy sauce, sugar, and chicken stock. Boil until liquid reduces and thickens to coat spoon. Season and serve. Serves 4.

YOGHURT AND SOY SAUCE MARINADE
MUSTARD SAUCE
FRIED BAMBOO SHOOTS
WITH MUSTARD GREENS*

Roast Pork
Roast Potatoes

YOGHURT AND SOY SAUCE MARINADE

1 c. yoghurt
½ c. soy sauce
2 tblsp. dry sherry (optional)

1 tsp. salt
Pepper

Mix all ingredients in bowl and marinate pork in the mixture for at least 6 hours or overnight. When ready to roast, scrape most of the mixture off. This should give the roast a crisp brown skin. The marinade is sufficient for a 4 to 5 pound pork loin.

MUSTARD SAUCE

1 c. cooking juices
1 tsp. cornstarch mixed with
1 tsp. water
2 tsp. dry mustard mixed with
2 tsp. water

1 tsp. soy sauce
2 tsp. dry sherry
(½ c. cream can be added in place of the soy sauce—this isn't really Chinese)
Salt and pepper

Bring cooking juices to boil. Add cornstarch and mustard mixtures. Stir for a few seconds. Add soy sauce and sherry. Boil until thickened.

Note: *If too thick add water.*

See Index for recipe for Fried Bamboo Shoots with Mustard Greens*.

PORK LOIN
BAKED BOSTON BEANS*

Baked Celery

This is a new way of cooking a pork loin. Instead of merely boiling and serving it, we boil it first, slice it, and quick-fry in a pan with ginger and scallions in the Chinese way.

Serve it with Baked Boston Beans* and bake the celery in the oven with the beans.

PORK LOIN

2 lbs. pork loin	2 cloves garlic, crushed
6 c. chicken stock	4 slices ginger, chopped
1 stalk celery	(or 1 tsp. powdered)
1 carrot	2 scallions, chopped
1 onion	¼ c. soy sauce
1 bay leaf	1 tsp. allspice
½ tsp. salt	2 tsp. sugar
2 tblsp. peanut or vegetable oil	1 tsp. chili sauce
	Pepper

Put the loin in a large pot. Add the stock, sliced celery, sliced carrot, sliced onion, bay leaf, and salt. Bring to boil and simmer for about 1 hour. Remove and drain, saving the stock for future use in other recipes. Slice the meat into strips about 2 inches long. Dry on paper towels.

In skillet heat oil. Add crushed garlic, chopped ginger, and chopped scallions. Stir-fry for 1 minute. Add meat and stir-fry for 3 minutes. Add soy sauce, allspice, sugar, chili sauce, and seasoning. Bring to boil and stir for 3 more minutes. Spoon over beans and serve immediately. Serves 4-6.

SWEET AND SOUR BEETS

Pork Sausages and Beans

Nothing could be more ordinary or all-American than pork and beans. And there's nothing much you can do to it, unless you find a dish that has a completely different taste, complements the beans, and doesn't fill you up to the bursting point. Here we suggest Sweet and Sour Beets, which you prepare just before the sausages and beans are ready. They only take about 15 minutes.

SWEET AND SOUR BEETS

6 small beets	3 tblsp. sugar
3 tblsp. peanut or vegetable oil	1½ c. cold water (or juice from canned beets)
1 tblsp. cornstarch mixed with	Salt and pepper
1 tblsp. water	3 tblsp. vinegar
	1 cup boiling water

Peel and slice beets. In skillet heat oil and sauté beets for 2 minutes. Remove from pan and drain on paper towels. Blend cornstarch mixture, sugar, 1½ cups cold water, and seasoning in a bowl. Pour into saucepan and add vinegar. Stir over low heat until it thickens and sugar is dissolved. Return beets to pan and pour sauce over them. Add boiling water. Stir until sauce is thick. Serves 4.

DUMPLINGS
CABBAGE WITH SWEET AND SOUR SAUCE

Baked Ham

You may think, as most people do, that it was the Italians who invented *pasta*. But the Chinese were eating noodles and ravioli before Marco Polo was old enough to walk. Later, when the news reached Italy, all they did was change the shape. The Chinese dumplings mentioned in this recipe are just like ravioli, but they're folded into little triangles instead of squares. You can fill them with anything you like, so you'll find they mix with practically any meal. Here we've suggested a meat filling and Cabbage with Sweet and Sour Sauce as a vegetable.

DUMPLINGS

2 c. flour	1 egg, beaten
1 tsp. salt	⅓ c. water

Start this when you've made the dough and are letting it stand.

½ lb. ground meat (any kind)	1 can (7 oz.) chicken broth
1 onion, grated	2 c. water
1 tsp. soy sauce	1 tsp. fresh minced parsley
1 tsp. dry sherry	Salt and pepper

Sift the flour and salt into a bowl. Stir in the egg and add water slowly, mixing lightly until a dough is formed. Don't use too much water. Knead on floured board. Let stand for 30 minutes.

Mix all ingredients for meat filling together in a bowl. When dough is ready, roll out and cut into 2 inch squares. Cover about 1 teaspoon of filling with a square of dough, folding it into a triangle. Bring soup to boil and drop dumplings in, a few at a time. Cook for 15 minutes. Serves 4.

CABBAGE WITH SWEET AND SOUR SAUCE

1 head firm white or green cabbage	2 tblsp. peanut or vegetable oil
1 c. Sweet and Sour Sauce*	Salt and pepper

Shred cabbage. Make Sweet and Sour Sauce* according to recipe listed in the Index. Heat oil in skillet. Add cabbage and stir-fry for 3 minutes. Season. Add sauce, bring to boil, and simmer for 2 minutes (if it begins to thicken remove from heat). Serves 4.

VEAL

The Chinese don't eat much veal and it is unlikely that you will come across it in a Chinese restaurant. However, it does lend itself well to the fast method of

Chinese cooking since this seals in its juices and keeps it tender. Veal also blends in with Chinese vegetables and rice.

Choose very pale flesh that is firm and fine. The paler the meat the better and more tender it is. The dark meat should be used in a stew or casserole.

STIR-FRIED LETTUCE WITH PEPPERS

Breaded Veal Cutlets
  Corn on the Cob

This meal makes use of the Chinese sense of color. It sets off the bright green of the peppers against the yellow of the corn. You could even shred a little red pepper over the green vegetables to add yet another color.

To improve the cutlets add a touch of Chinese Hot Mustard* or soy sauce to the bread crumbs.

STIR-FRIED LETTUCE WITH PEPPERS

1 head lettuce (any kind)	1 tsp. soy sauce
2 green peppers, washed and seeded	Salt and pepper
2 tblsp. peanut or vegetable oil	

Wash the larger leaves of the lettuce (save the smaller ones for use in a salad). Dry them thoroughly. Chop the peppers and parboil for 1 or 2 minutes. Drain. In skillet heat oil. Add peppers and stir-fry for 2 minutes. Add lettuce and stir-fry for 1 minute. Add soy sauce and seasoning. Serve at once. Serves 4.

Veal Chops
  Potatoes or Rice

The chops will be juicier if you brown
top of the stove, then cover them, and let them simmer for about 15-20 minutes. Scrape up their juices
into a sauce after they are cooked. You could boil
juices down with a little wine and herbs.

The mixed vegetable dish can contain any vegetable you wish, including leftovers, which can be added
at the end. This is a typical Chinese method and rela-
tively unknown in any other school of cooking.

MIXED VEGETABLES III

½ c. cauliflower flowerets	½ c. chopped fresh
½ c. peas	mushrooms
3 tblsp. peanut or vegeta-	½ tsp. salt
ble oil	½ c. chicken stock
3 slices ginger, chopped	1 tsp. Tabasco sauce
½ c. chopped celery	Pepper
½ c. chopped endive	

Parboil cauliflower. Thaw peas if using frozen. In
skillet heat oil. Add ginger and stir-fry for 1 minute.
Add cauliflower and stir-fry for 2 minutes. Add celery
and endive. Stir-fry 1 minute. Add peas and
mushrooms. Stir-fry for 2 minutes. Add salt. Bring
stock to boil and add to pan. Add Tabasco, seasoning,
and cook for 2 more minutes, covered. Serves 4.

BAMBOO SHOOTS AND CHILI SAUCE*
FRIED RICE*

Veal Chops

Buy good large chops and season them with lemon juice, salt, and pepper before you cook them.

You will need two skillets for the vegetables, so a good way to cook the chops would be in a covered casserole in the oven. First brown the chops on top of the stove in a tablespoon each oil and butter and then put them in the oven (about 350° F.) until they are done (about 30 minutes). When they are almost ready, start the vegetables. Do the necessary chopping while the meat is cooking.

Remember that the shoots must be thoroughly dry before they are fried. Consult the Index to locate the Fried Rice* and Fried Bamboo Shoots and Chili Sauce*.

SAUTEED ROMAINE LETTUCE
RICE AND MUSHROOMS*

Veal Scallops

Pound the veal scallops with the flat side of a knife. Remove any white filament. Cook the veal very fast in a tablespoon each butter and oil over a high flame. Remove to a side dish and scrape up the cooking juices. Add a tablespoon lemon juice and 2 tablespoons white wine for 4 6-ounce scallops.

Place the mushrooms and rice in a serving dish and put the veal on top. Spoon the sauce over and serve. Start the lettuce when you have finished everything else. It only takes about a minute to cook.

SAUTÉED ROMAINE LETTUCE

1 lb. romaine lettuce
5 tblsp. peanut or vegetable oil

1 clove garlic, crushed
1 tsp. salt
Pepper

Wash, drain, and dry the lettuce thoroughly. Heat oil in skillet. Add garlic and salt. When brown add lettuce and seasoning; stir-fry for 1 minute. Serve at once. Serves 4.

Note: *You can use the same recipe for any other lettuce.*

STRING BEANS AND BAMBOO SHOOTS

Veal Stew
Potatoes or Noodles

This is a typical casserole dinner served with a Chinese side dish. When the stew and potatoes or noodles are ready to serve, cook the vegetables. If fresh beans are used, slice them into 2 inch pieces.

STRING BEANS AND BAMBOO SHOOTS

1 lb. fresh or 1 pkg. (10 oz.) frozen beans, thawed
1 can (5 oz.) bamboo shoots

3 tblsp. peanut or vegetable oil
¼ tsp. sugar
¾ c. chicken stock or water
Salt and pepper

Drain and dry beans and bamboo shoots. Heat oil in skillet. Add beans and cook for 5 minutes over high heat, stirring constantly. Add bamboo shoots, sugar, and stock. Bring to boil. Simmer for 7 minutes. Season and serve. Serves 4. (Drain any remaining liquid.)

SNOW PEAS AND MUSHROOMS

Veal Scallops
Noodles

This meal is very delicately flavored. A light white wine would go very well with it.

Choose the palest pink flesh possible for the scallops. Flatten them with a knife before you cook them. After they are cooked remove them to a side dish and add lemon juice and cream to the pan. Serve the scallops over the noodles with the sauce on top. It is almost essential to have a sauce over the scallops—it brings out their flavor.

SNOW PEAS AND MUSHROOMS

6 Chinese dried mushrooms, soaked in water overnight (or for 30 min.)
1 lb. fresh or 1 pkg. (10 oz.) frozen snow peas, thawed
4 scallions
3 tblsp. peanut or vegetable oil
3 slices ginger, chopped (or ½ tsp. powdered)
½ c. chicken stock
1 tsp. cornstarch mixed with
1 tsp. water
Salt and pepper

Drain mushrooms. Trim snow peas if fresh and chop scallions. Heat 1 tablespoon oil in skillet. Fry ginger and scallions for 2 minutes. Add mushrooms; stir-fry for 1 minute. Add stock; bring to boil. Add cornstarch mixture and simmer for 2 minutes. In another skillet heat rest of oil. Fry snow peas for 2 minutes. Transfer to side dish. Pour mushrooms over peas and serve. Serves 4.

VEAL WITH CELERY

Vermicelli
  Spinach

Veal is rarely used in China but it is so popular in the United States that it would have been absurd not to try it in a Chinese way. And indeed it lends itself very well to the Chinese style of cooking.

Here we pan-fry it and serve it with vermicelli (replacing the thin Chinese ones) and spinach. Don't cook the vermicelli until the veal is cooked. These thin noodles are very delicate and must not be overcooked.

Grate a little nutmeg over the spinach before you serve it.

VEAL WITH CELERY

1 lb. stewing veal	1 tsp. water
2 tblsp. soy sauce	1 bunch celery
3 tblsp. dry sherry	6 tblsp. peanut or vegetable oil
1 tsp. cornstarch mixed with	Salt and pepper

Cut the veal into 1 inch cubes. Dredge with soy sauce, 1 tablespoon sherry, and cornstarch mixture. Remove celery leaves and tough parts and save for future use in making stock. Chop rest of celery and parboil. Drain and dry. In skillet heat oil. Fry the veal lightly until browned. Add celery, rest of sherry, and seasoning. Cook for 2 more minutes. Season and serve immediately. Serves 4.

VEAL WITH MUSHROOMS
FRIED SNOW PEAS*

Noodles or Rice

This is a Chinese stew and it is simmered on top of the stove for about 1½ hours. We suggest a fried Chinese vegetable to go with it because it is easy to fry at the last minute.

Use the water from the soaked mushrooms with your stock. It will give it a delicious flavor.

VEAL WITH MUSHROOMS

2 lbs. veal
3 tblsp. peanut or vegetable oil
3 scallions
2 cloves garlic
1 tsp. anise seeds
2 slices ginger, chopped

2 c. chicken stock
1 c. mushroom water
8 Chinese dried mushrooms, soaked overnight (or for 30 min.)
Salt and pepper

Cut veal into 1 inch cubes. In skillet heat oil. Sauté veal lightly until browned and remove to side dish. Chop scallions, crush garlic, and add, with anise seeds and ginger, to oil. Fry for 2 minutes. Return veal to pan. Heat stock and add, with mushroom water, to pan. Bring to boil and simmer for 1 hour, until veal is nearly done. Add drained mushrooms, season, and simmer for about half an hour. Season. Serves 4.

VEAL WITH BEAN SPROUTS

Mashed Potatoes
Cauliflower

Prepare all your ingredients for the Chinese dish while the vegetables are cooking. When they are done, put them in heated dishes and keep them warm in the oven while you cook the veal dish. You can keep foods cooked the American way warm in the oven without spoiling them, but you cannot do this with Chinese food.

VEAL WITH BEAN SPROUTS

1 lb. veal
1 can (5 oz.) bean sprouts
3 tblsp. peanut or vegetable oil
1 clove garlic, crushed
2 scallions
1 slice ginger, chopped

3 tblsp. soy sauce
1 tblsp. dry sherry
1 tsp. cornstarch mixed with
1 tsp. water
Salt and pepper

Cut veal into paper-thin strips. Drain bean sprouts. In skillet heat oil. Crush garlic, chop scallions, and add with ginger to oil. Stir-fry for 1 minute. Add veal and stir-fry for 1 minute. Add bean sprouts; stir-fry 2 minutes. Add soy sauce, sherry, and cornstarch mixture. Cook until sauce coats spoon. Season and serve immediately. Serves 4.

BUFFET

There are two main points to keep in mind when serving a buffet dinner. One is the appearance of the food. Dull, unimaginative spreads of baked hams, turkeys, and salads turn off rather than stimulate the appetite. The Chinese are experts in serving food and know how to make a table look interesting, by contrasting colors—the whiteness of rice against the bright green of vegetables, the golden tone of a soup against a rich, dark meat, and punctuating the spread with different color dips set round the table.

The other point to keep in mind is contrast of textures and flavors—serve a smooth sauce with a crunchy duck, sweet with sour, salty with pungent. The dips mentioned at the beginning of the chapter add new and unusual flavors to a buffet, as well as making the table attractive and different.

BUFFET DIPS

These dips should be put in little dishes (buy small, inexpensive Chinese dishes. They are the same size as a saucer.) and set out on the table for people to help themselves. Make several for a buffet dinner and vary color, taste, and texture.

Chinese Mustard* with Sour Cream

(Goes with chicken, beef, lamb, liver and pork.)

2 tblsp. Chinese Mustard*	Salt and pepper
6 tblsp. sour cream	

Mix together and serve. Makes about 2 dishes.

Soy Sauce with Pimiento

(Goes with chicken, turkey, lamb, and shellfish.)

4 tblsp. soy sauce
1 small jar pimientos, drained

Place soy sauce in bowl. Chop pimientos finely and add. Mix together and serve. Makes about 2 dishes.

Horseradish Dip

(Goes with fish, beef, and lamb.)

2 tsp. horseradish	2 tsp. grated fresh ginger
½ onion	(or 1 tsp. powder)
4 radishes	2 rashers bacon, cooked

Place horseradish in bowl. Grate onion, radishes, and ginger and add to bowl. Chop bacon. Add to bowl. Mix all ingredients together and serve. Makes about 2 dishes.

Note: *You can add 2 teaspoons sour cream to this dip for variation.*

Avocado and Bean Sprout Dip

(Goes with all fowl, meat, and fish.)

1 avocado, seeded and pitted	1 egg yolk
	½ can (5 oz.) bean sprouts
2 tblsp. mayonnaise	Salt and pepper

In bowl mash avocado. Add mayonnaise and egg yolk. Drain bean sprouts, mince, and add with seasoning to bowl. Mix together and serve. Makes about 2 dishes.

Mushroom and Butter Dip

(Goes with all fowl, meat, and fish.)

4 Chinese dried mushrooms, soaked in water overnight (or for 30 min.)	3 scallion tops or chives, (optional)
	Salt and pepper
4 oz. (1 stick) whipped butter	

Drain and finely chop mushrooms. Mix in bowl with butter. If desired, add scallion tops, finely chopped, or chives. Whip together with fork. Serve. Makes about 2 dishes.

Note: *This is excellent over a steak. Make the butter mixture into patties and refrigerate until ready for use. Put on top of steaks and serve.*

Hot Chili Dip

(Goes with shrimp and all meats, especially beef, duck, and lamb.)

2 cloves garlic	½ cup soy sauce
2 tsp. Tabasco sauce	1 tsp. sugar
1 chili pepper	

Crush garlic. Mix with Tabasco. Chop chili pepper finely. Add to mixture with soy sauce and sugar. Mix well and turn into dip dishes. Makes about 2 dishes.

Garlic and Oil Dip

(Goes with all fowl and shellfish.)

3 tblsp. peanut or vegetable oil	2 cloves garlic
3 tblsp. soy sauce	3 slices ginger

Mix oil and soy sauce. Crush garlic and chop ginger very fine. Mix together and pour into dip dishes. Makes about 2 dishes.

GARNISHES

The following ingredients, chopped up and scattered over buffet dishes, add flavor, texture, and color to the buffet table. Use your imagination and search out new garnishes from leftovers, vegetables, etc.

walnuts
cashew nuts
almonds
peanuts
mushrooms
scallion tops
dried shrimp
diced fresh shrimp
bamboo shoots
parsley
sesame seeds
rice noodles
ham
lettuce
fried eggs,
   omelet style   } cut in narrow strips

BARBECUED BEEF ROLLS WITH CHINESE STUFFING

Instead of turning out the usual grilled steaks on your barbecue, try rolled stuffed steak. They're beautifully tender—and foolproof. The only trouble is keeping the steaks rolled tight as you cook them. If they seem to come apart, pin the meat together with a toothpick.

2 small onions, diced	2 c. cooked rice
½ lb. chopped mushrooms	2 tblsp. sherry
1 tsp. peanut or vegetable oil	1 tsp. dry mustard
1 tsp. ginger powder	Salt and pepper
½ c. mashed black beans	8 thin-sliced cubed steaks
2 tblsp. soy sauce	8 rashers bacon

Fry onions and mushrooms lightly in oil, until the onions are clear. In bowl mix ginger, black beans, soy sauce, rice, sherry, mustard, and seasoning. Mix in mushrooms and onions. Put about 2 tablespoons mixture in each steak. Wrap meat around it and wrap bacon over the meat. Turn frequently over grill until bacon is browned. Serves 4.

CORNISH HENS BARBECUED CHINESE STYLE

This is a lavish item for a buffet dinner. Allow half a hen per person. The hens are roasted in the oven, or on a barbecue, and basted with pineapple and apricot juice colored with red food coloring. This is a Chinese custom with some roasted foods and it adds color and variety to the table. Surround it with white rice and green peas and serve with Sweet and Sour Sauce*.

4 Cornish hens	1 jar (4½ oz.) baby food apricot purée
3 tblsp. peanut or vegetable oil	1 tsp. red food coloring
½ c. pineapple juice	Salt and pepper

Thaw the hens out overnight (if they are frozen). Wash and dry them. Preheat oven to 350° F. In a bowl mix together oil, pineapple juice, apricot purée, and food coloring. Season hens with salt and pepper. Spread a little of the mixture over them. Place them on barbecue spit or in oven and baste with mixture every 15 minutes until they are cooked. They are done when the juices run clear and yellow. Serves 8 (half a hen each).

CHINESE HAM

It is unlikely that you will find a genuine Chinese ham in a local butcher shop, but a two-year-old Smithfield ham is the closest substitute. It is the flavoring that makes the difference, and ham with a Chinese accent is a welcome change from the usual dull buffet hams that are served up over and over again.

5 lbs. ham	½ tsp. anise powder
8 scallions	½ c. dry sherry
1 large leek	1 tblsp. brown sugar
2 c. chicken stock	3 cloves garlic, crushed
1 tsp. powdered ginger	2 cloves
2 c. soy sauce	Water to cover ham

Wash ham and dry with paper towels. Chop scallions; clean and slice leek. In a large pot bring stock to boil. Add scallions, leek, ginger, soy sauce, anise powder, sherry, sugar, garlic, and cloves. Add ham and enough water to stock to cover. Bring to boil, cover, and simmer for 3 hours or until tender. Serve hot or cold. Serves 12.

FRIED OYSTERS AND EGGPLANT

This is a fascinating dish. The eggplant is cut into pieces exactly the same size as the oysters. Both the eggplant and oysters are dipped into the batter and fried. They are strangely similar in taste, if not in texture. It makes an excellent buffet dish because it will stretch to a lot of people.

Serve with a dip of tartar sauce, Duk (or Plum) Sauce*, or a mixture of wine, Tabasco sauce, and Chinese Hot Mustard*.

2 pints oysters	6 tblsp. cornstarch
2 eggplants	1½ c. water
2 tblsp. white wine	2 eggs
Salt	5 c. peanut or vegetable
2 c. flour	oil for deep-frying
2 tsp. baking powder	

Wash oysters in salt water, parboil in clear water for 1 minute. Peel and cut eggplants into cubes oyster-size. Salt and let stand. Dredge oysters in wine and salt. Mix sifted flour, baking powder, cornstarch, water, and eggs. Coat the oysters and eggplant with the mixture. In skillet heat oil. Deep-fry ingredients until golden brown. Drain on paper towels. Turn into chafing dish and serve. Serves 8-10.

BARBECUED PORK

This is excellent for a party because very little work is required on the evening it is served. If you have a barbecue spit, you simply reheat the pork over the coals. We cook it beforehand in the oven.

This method can be used for barbecued chicken and beef, Chinese style.

2 lbs. pork tenderloin	½ c. soy sauce
½ c. orange juice	Salt and pepper

Soak the pork overnight in mixture of orange juice, soy sauce, and seasoning. Preheat oven to 450° F. Place pork on rack with a pan underneath to catch drippings and cook for 15 minutes to the pound. Turn oven down to 300° F. and cook for half an hour.

When you are ready to eat simply reheat the pork over the coals. This way you won't run the risk of eating undercooked pork, which can be dangerous.

Sauce

½ c. tomato paste	Salt and pepper
½ c. dry sherry	

Bring the tomato paste and sherry to a boil. Season and serve as dip for pork.

You can also try Sweet and Sour Sauce*, Duk (Plum) Sauce* to which you might add 1 tablespoon applesauce or plain soy sauce.

SWEET AND SOUR PORKBALLS

This is a very good dish for the sweet and sour part of a buffet. The pork balls must be kept warm however, so you will need a chafing dish on the table. Cover them with the sauce and keep it gently heating all the time.

2 lbs. ground pork (or 1 lb. ground pork and 1 lb. sausage meat)
8 scallions, chopped
4 tblsp. soy sauce
4 tblsp. dry sherry
2 eggs
2 tblsp. chopped parsley
1 tsp. powdered ginger
6 tblsp. cornstarch mixed with
2 tblsp. water

2 tsp. salt
1 tsp. pepper
5 c. peanut or vegetable oil
1 can (1 lb.) diced carrots, drained
2 sweet red peppers
1 pkg. (10 oz.) frozen snow peas, thawed
8 tblsp. sugar
6 tblsp. white wine vinegar
1 tsp. Tabasco sauce
1 c. chicken stock

Note: *Watch for measurements; we add half the amount of some ingredients to the pork balls and the other half to the sauce later.*

In a large mixing bowl combine the pork (or sausage meat), scallions, 2 tablespoons soy sauce, 2 tablespoons sherry, eggs, parsley, ginger, half the cornstarch mixture, and seasoning. Make the mixture into balls golf-ball size. Heat oil in skillet. Deep-fry the balls until browned. Drain on paper towels.

Empty out all but 2 tablespoons oil. Stir-fry carrots, peppers, and snow peas for 3 minutes. In bowl mix 2 tablespoons soy sauce, 2 tablespoons sherry, sugar, vinegar, and Tabasco. Pour over vegetables, add stock, and bring to boil. Add remaining cornstarch mixture. Cook until sauce coats spoon. Add pork balls and turn mixture into chafing dish. Serves 10-12.

DEEP-FRIED SHRIMP WITH PINEAPPLE

Leave the tails on the shrimp so that people can pick them up with their fingers and dip them into the sauce. Put toothpicks in the pineapple. Set out dishes of soy sauce, Duk (Plum) Sauce*, and Chinese Hot Mustard*.

1 lb. shrimp
1 c. flour
1 tsp. salt
2 eggs
¼ to ½ c. water (or beer)
1 tsp. dry sherry
4 c. peanut or vegetable oil
1 tblsp. cornstarch mixed with

1 tblsp. water
1 tblsp. brown sugar
4 tblsp. vinegar
½ c. pineapple juice (use juice from canned chunks)
Salt and pepper
1 can (1 lb.) pineapple chunks

Clean and devein the shrimp, leaving the tails on. Sift the flour and salt into a bowl, beat the eggs and add them. Add water and sherry. Mix together and dip shrimp into the batter so that they are coated. In deep-frying pan heat oil to bubbling point. Deep-fry the shrimp until golden and drain on paper towels.

Mix together cornstarch mixture, sugar, vinegar, and pineapple juice. Cook over low heat until thickened. Season and add the pineapple chunks. Heat through and serve shrimp in another dish. Serves 4-6.

BARBECUED SHRIMP

The shrimp can be baked in the oven, grilled, or sprinkled with charcoal powder and skewered over a barbecue pit. Brush with the sauce constantly if you do it the latter way.

Break the backs of the shrimp before you cook them so that they won't curl up. If you are serving them on a buffet table, put them in a chafing dish to keep hot.

When buying shrimp for this dish, choose the

larger ones. The small ones are good for sauces but do not grill well.

1 lb. shrimp	2 tblsp. soy sauce
2 slices ginger, chopped	2 tblsp. brown sugar
1 tsp. ginger powder	1 tblsp. peanut or vegeta-
1 tsp. tomato purée	ble oil
4 scallions, finely chopped	Salt and pepper
2 tblsp. dry sherry	

Clean the shrimp, but leave their tails and shells on. In a bowl mix all the other ingredients. Marinate the shrimp in the mixture for at least an hour. Remove from mixture and either bake at 350° F., grill, or barbecue for 10 minutes. If you barbecue the shrimp, brush with charcoal powder, cook, and squeeze a lemon over them before serving. Serves 4.

SHRIMP BALLS WITH WATER CHESTNUTS

Keep the shrimp balls warm in a chafing dish on the table. Either make a hot sauce (such as Oyster Sauce*, Sweet and Sour Sauce*) and spoon it over the shrimp balls, or use a bottled sauce as a dip. See the Index for sauce ideas.

A blender would be very helpful for this recipe. You can put all the ingredients in it and grind them, instead of spending time chopping everything.

2 lbs. fresh shrimp	2 tsp. chili powder
2 cans (5 oz.) water chest-	2 tsp. Duk (Plum) Sauce*
nuts, drained	4 tblsp. cornstarch
3 tblsp. soy sauce	4 eggs
2 tblsp. dry sherry	1 tsp. salt
2 cloves garlic, crushed	½ tsp. pepper
3 slices fresh ginger (or 1	6 c. peanut or vegetable
tsp. powdered)	oil for deep-frying

Clean and dice shrimp. Chop chestnuts. (If you have a blender, put them in it whole and grind them.) In bowl or blender mix all ingredients except oil. Make them into balls golf-ball size. Heat oil in skillet. Deep-fry the shrimp balls until they are golden brown. Put half of them into a chafing dish and set on the table. Keep the other half warm in the oven. Serves 10-12.

STEWED TONGUE

The tongue will have a completely different flavor when cooked this way. You can serve it either hot or cold, with Chinese Hot Mustard* and Duk (Plum) Sauce*. Garnish the dish with parsley.

Choose a short cut of tongue, there will be more meat on it. Boil it for 3 or 4 hours and peel the skin off.

4 lb. tongue	3 ginger slices
1 stalk celery	¼ c. soy sauce
1 onion, coarsely chopped	2 tsp. salt
1 chicken bouillon cube	Pepper
1 qt. water	

Put the tongue, together with celery, onion, and bouillon cube in the water. Bring to boil and add ginger slices, soy sauce, and seasoning. Simmer for 3 to 4 hours, until tender. Drain, peel, and serve hot or cold. Serves 6-8.

KEBAB CHICKEN BREASTS CHINESE STYLE

The flavor achieved here is quite different from the usual shish kebab. The ingredients are marinated for at least an hour before cooking, grilled or baked for about 20 minutes, and served either on the skewer or removed and placed on a large plate. They can be removed from the marinade and placed in the oven

196

when your guests arrive. Thus without any more fuss they will be ready when you are.

8 chicken breasts	½ c. soy sauce
6 green peppers	4 tblsp. dry sherry
½ lb. large white mushrooms	4 slices ginger, chopped
2 cans (5 oz.) water chest-nuts, drained	2 tsp. Chinese Hot Mustard*
	Salt and pepper

Bone and pound the chicken breasts and cut them into pieces 1½ inches square. Seed and cut the peppers to the same size. Remove stalks from mushrooms. Slice water chestnuts in half vertically. Thread ingredients on skewers. In wide dish mix soy sauce, sherry, ginger, mustard, and seasoning. Soak the skewers in the mixture for an hour. Remove and either bake (in preheated 350° F. oven) or grill for 20 minutes, until chicken is cooked. Serves 10.

ROAST TURKEY I

Turkey can be one of the most boring items possible at a buffet, but here it is simmered in aromatic herbs and spices, roasted in the oven, and sprinkled with sesame seeds. Duk (Plum) Sauce* would be a good accompaniment.

8-10 lb. turkey	1½ tsp. salt
6 slices ginger root	1½ tsp. pepper
6 scallion stalks, chopped	10 c. water (more if needed)
3 c. soy sauce	
1 c. dry sherry	2 tblsp. peanut or vegetable oil
2 tblsp. brown sugar	
1 tsp. thyme	2 tblsp. sesame seeds
1 bay leaf	

Wash and dry turkey. In a large pan combine ginger, scallions, soy sauce, sherry, sugar, thyme, bay leaf, and seasoning. Bring to boil with water. Add turkey. Bring to boil, turn down heat, and simmer for 45 minutes to an hour. Preheat oven to 350° F. Remove turkey from pan and place on roasting rack. Roast for an hour, basting with the stock liquid. Sprinkle with oil and seeds. Turn oven to 450° F. and cook until turkey is browned. Serves 15-20.

ROAST TURKEY II

Here are two very unusual stuffings for turkey. If you are feeling especially adventurous you might make half the amount of both and stuff them in opposite ends of the same turkey.

The sauce here goes well with both stuffings. Fry the giblets, chopped in small pieces, in butter and add them to the sauce.

8-10 lb. turkey

Stuffing I

½ lb. ham, cooked and diced

½ lb. chicken livers, cooked and diced

½ can (5 oz.) bamboo shoots, diced

½ c. diced celery

2 tblsp. chopped celery leaves

4 Chinese dried mushrooms, soaked in water overnight (or for 30 min.) and diced

1 c. boiled and diced chestnuts

2 tsp. ginger powder

2 tblsp. soy sauce

1 tsp. brown sugar

1 c. cooked rice

Salt and pepper

Note: *All these ingredients can be put in a blender and minced together. It will save a lot of time.*

Preheat oven to 300° F. Wash the turkey and wipe the inside with paper towels. Mix all the ingredients together in a bowl or blender. Stuff turkey and cook for 25 minutes to the pound.

Stuffing II

1 can (3¾ oz.) smoked oysters, diced
1 small eggplant, peeled and diced
2 tsp. chopped celery leaves
½ c. diced celery
2 tsp. ginger powder
2 tblsp. soy sauce
1 onion, diced
2 tblsp. dry sherry
1 tsp. sugar
Salt and pepper
1 c. bread crumbs or cooked rice

Preheat oven to 300° F. Wash the turkey and wipe inside with paper towels. Mix all ingredients together in bowl or blender. Stuff turkey and bake for 25 minutes to the pound.

Note: *You may add 4 cooked, chopped rashers of bacon to this stuffing.*

Sauce

Turkey giblets, chopped and fried
1 clove garlic, crushed
2 slices ginger, chopped
2 tblsp. soy sauce
½ can (5 oz.) bean sprouts, drained (optional)
1 tsp. cornstarch mixed with
1 tsp. water
½ c. dry sherry
1 c. turkey stock (or chicken)
Salt and pepper

Mix sauce ingredients in bowl. Heat in small pan until the sauce reduces to coat the spoon. Serve in heated sauceboat. Yields about 1 cup.

SIDE DISHES

CHINESE STYLE BEANS

Beans are inexpensive, simple to prepare, and are very good in a buffet because they will keep hot if you serve them in a large casserole dish.

Here are two recipes for beans, one for canned beans improved with Chinese flavorings and another for soy beans soaked overnight and baked in the oven with spices.

Boston Baked Beans

2 cans (1 lb.) Boston baked beans	3 scallion tops
1 stalk celery	1 tblsp. soy sauce
1 onion	1 tsp. dry mustard

Preheat oven to 350° F. Place beans in large casserole. Chop celery, onion, and scallion tops finely and add to beans. Add soy sauce, mustard and bake in the oven for about 20 minutes, until thoroughly heated. Serves 8.

Baked Soy Beans

1 c. soy beans	1 tblsp. soy sauce
4 slices ginger	Salt and pepper
1 onion	

Soak soy beans overnight and drain. Preheat oven to 300° F. Chop up ginger and onion. Place beans, ginger, and onion plus soy sauce and seasoning in casserole. Bake for an hour, or until beans are tender and cooked through. Serves 8.

Note: *These bean casseroles can be improved by the addition of pork leftovers, diced, or other meat leftovers.*

EGGS HARD-BOILED WITH TEA LEAVES

The eggs are boiled in water, run under the cold tap, and the shells are cracked with a spoon. You then add the tea and seasonings to the water and boil the eggs for another 10 minutes. When you take the shells off you will have an attractive pattern which will look very well on a buffet table. You can add to this by putting different vegetable colorings in the water too.

10 eggs	2 tblsp. salt
2 tsp. mint	1 tblsp. black pepper
4 tblsp. strong dark tea	

Boil eggs for 10 minutes. Run under cold tap and crack shells. To water add mint, tea, and seasoning. Boil eggs for 10 more minutes. Run under cold tap, peel, and serve.

Note: *In second boiling add vegetable coloring if desired. (This is good for Easter time.)*

STUFFED CHINESE CABBAGE

It is unlikely that you will be able to find a genuine Chinese cabbage in your supermarket, but you will see that an ordinary green cabbage does equally well. Roll the leaves over the stuffing in the same manner as for stuffing vine leaves.

Here are three different ways of serving stuffed cabbage at a buffet: cold, with lemon; hot, stuffed with rice and cashew nuts; and hot, with a sauce.

Stuffing I

10 large cabbage leaves	1 tsp. soy sauce
¼ lb. ground pork	1 tsp. cornstarch
4 chopped scallions	Salt and pepper

Parboil cabbage leaves; drain and dry. Cut into shapes 5 inches long and 2 inches wide. Make three incisions in the leaves. Mix remaining ingredients together in bowl and place a portion on each leaf. Wrap the leaves over the ingredients and press down tightly. Put in a greased pot, cover with lid or foil paper, set on rack in two inches of boiling water, and steam for 15 minutes. Reserve juice for use in sauce. Serve either cold, with lemon juice, or hot, with the following sauce. Serves 5 (2 each).

Sauce

1 c. vegetable juice, from cabbage after steaming (or 1 c. chicken stock)	2 tblsp. brown sugar
	2 tsp. cornstarch mixed with
1 tblsp. soy sauce	2 tsp. sherry
1 tblsp. vinegar	Salt and pepper

In small pan bring all ingredients to a boil, and cook until the sauce thickens to coat the spoon. Either serve separately or pour over leaves and serve in chafing dish.

Stuffing II

10 large cabbage leaves	½ c. cooked rice
¼ lb. ground cashew nuts (use blender to grind)	1 tsp. soy sauce
4 scallions, chopped	1 tsp. cornstarch
	Salt and pepper

Parboil leaves, mix all other ingredients, and proceed as in Stuffing I. You may use the same sauce to serve with the leaves.

PORK-STUFFED PEPPERS

These peppers are very good with a buffet. To make them go further, cut them in half after you have cooked them, sprinkle them with paprika for decoration, and serve on a plate. You can also scatter a few finely chopped scallion tops over the halves.

If you choose to make the stock liquid into a sauce,

serve it separately in a heated sauceboat. It will not be good if it gets cold on the table.

8 green peppers	1 can (5 oz.) water chestnuts, drained and chopped
1 lb. ground pork	
4 scallions, chopped	
6 Chinese dried mushrooms, soaked in water overnight (or for 30 min.), drained and chopped	3 tsp. chopped cashew nuts (optional)
	2 tblsp. soy sauce
	2 tsp. peanut or vegetable oil
	Salt and pepper
	2 c. chicken stock

For Sauce

1 tblsp. soy sauce	2 tsp. dry sherry
2 tsp. cornstarch mixed with	

Remove tops, wash and seed peppers. In bowl mix pork with chopped scallions, chopped mushrooms, and chopped water chestnuts. Add chopped cashew nuts. (All this chopping can be avoided if you have a blender.) Add soy sauce, oil, and seasoning, and mix together. Stuff peppers with mixture. In skillet bring stock to boil. Add peppers, cover and cook for 1 hour over low heat. When the peppers are done, remove to plate. Boil down stock to 1 cup. Add soy sauce and cornstarch-sherry mixture. Boil until sauce coats the spoon. Turn into heated sauceboat and serve. Serves 8-16 (depending on whether you halve them or not).

CHINESE WONTONS

This is a short-cut idea for making Chinese Wontons for use in soups, or served separately in dish with a buffet dinner. You can vary the fillings. In fact it would be exciting to use different fillings and mix them up on the plate so that they are a surprise. You can freeze these and use them as you need.

1 package biscuit dough

Filling

Diced shrimp	Minced clams
Diced lobster	Chopped leftover meat
Rice and herbs	Diced parsley
Mashed soy beans	Peanut or vegetable oil for
Chopped mixed vegetables	deep-frying
(leftovers)	

Make the biscuit dough according to the directions on the package. Spread it out into a thin layer. Cut squares and wrap around filling, like ravioli. Deep-fry in oil until golden color. Drain on paper towels. To serve either put them in a chafing dish, or serve floating in hot chicken broth and spoon out like dumplings. Serves 8.

BAKED FRIED RICE

Fry the rice ahead of time and reheat in the oven an hour before you are due to eat. We suggest here additions of peppers and mushrooms, which can be added not only for flavor but for decoration.

4 c. cooked Fried Rice*	4 Chinese dried
1 green pepper	mushrooms, soaked in
1 red pepper	water overnight (or for
	30 minutes), drained
	Salt and pepper

Preheat oven to 300° F. Place rice in bowl. Seed and chop peppers and mushrooms very finely, and mix them, with the seasoning, in with the rice. Place in covered casserole and heat in low oven for about an hour, or until heated through. Serves 8.

Note: *Vary this dish by adding drained chopped bean sprouts, ginger, pimiento, leftover meat, etc. It is an excellent way of using up leftovers.*

CHINESE PICKLED CABBAGE

This is excellent as a variation from the usual cole slaw. You can use Chinese cabbage (if available), or green or red cabbage in this recipe. You might even mix two colors.

2 lbs. round cabbage	1 tsp. Chinese Hot Mustard*
2 tblsp. brown sugar	
1 tsp. candied ginger, pounded (if available)	2 tblsp. soy sauce
	1 tsp. salt
3 tblsp. vinegar	Pepper
1 tsp. Tabasco sauce	3 tblsp. peanut or vegetable oil

Remove outer leaves of cabbage. Core and chop into 1 inch cubes. In bowl mix together sugar, ginger, vinegar, Tabasco, mustard, soy sauce, and seasoning. Heat oil in skillet. Quick-fry cabbage until clear and crisp. Remove from pan. Add mixture, bring to boil, and cook for 2 minutes. Pour over cabbage, toss and refrigerate overnight. Serves 6-8.

BEAN SPROUT AND WATERCRESS SALAD

This goes especially well with lamb dishes and barbecued meats. Add the dressing just before you serve it, not earlier or else the watercress leaves will become soggy.

2 cans (5 oz.) bean sprouts	3 tsp. peanut or vegetable oil
1 bunch watercress	
1 tsp. sugar	Salt and pepper
1 tsp. vinegar	2 tsp. soy sauce

Drain bean sprouts. Wash and dry watercress, removing the tougher parts of the stems. In a cup mix together the rest of the ingredients and refrigerate. When ready pour over vegetables, toss and serve. Serves 6-8.

CHINESE CUCUMBER SALAD

Here are two recipes for cucumber salad. The first is entirely Chinese and the second is a combination of Chinese and Western. Grate the cucumber into thin slivers with a potato peeler. It will absorb the dressing more quickly and thoroughly. Add the dressing immediately and let the cucumber stand in it for an hour or so to soak it all in.

Dressing I

2 slices ginger, chopped (or 1 tsp. powder)
2 tblsp. sugar
4 tblsp. vinegar

2 large cucumbers
2 scallion tops, finely minced
Salt and pepper

In a saucepan combine the ginger, sugar, and vinegar and heat until the sugar has been absorbed. Peel and sliver the cucumbers. Let the dressing cool, pour it over the cucumbers. Scatter the minced scallion tops over the mixture, season and toss. Refrigerate for 1 hour. Serves 4.

Dressing II

2 cloves garlic
2 tblsp. soy sauce
6 tblsp. yoghurt
2 tsp. peanut or vegetable oil

Salt and pepper
2 large cucumbers

Crush garlic and mix in bowl with other ingredients except cucumbers. Peel and sliver cucumber. Toss in dressing, refrigerate for an hour, and serve. Serves 4.

MUSHROOM SALAD

Choose good, white fresh mushrooms; remove the stems and slice the mushrooms thinly so that they will absorb the dressing easily. This dish is very similar to mushrooms *à la Grecque* but we have added Chinese flavors to it. You can also serve this salad as an hors d'oeuvre.

1 lb. mushrooms	2 tblsp. vinegar
1 onion	2 tblsp. peanut or vegeta-ble oil
1 tblsp. sugar	
1 tblsp. soy sauce	Salt and pepper
2 tblsp. dry sherry	1 tsp. chopped parsley

Wash, dry, and slice mushrooms thinly, removing the stems. Shred the onion. In saucepan combine onion, sugar, soy sauce, sherry, and vinegar. Bring to boil. Remove from heat and pour over mushrooms. Add oil, seasoning, and parsley. Toss, refrigerate for a day, and serve. Serves 4 as a salad.

LEFTOVERS

One of the great joys of Chinese cooking lies in the fact that there is absolutely no waste. The Chinese never throw anything away and some of their best dishes are made from leftovers. In fact they often plan meals with leftovers in mind. Even a small amount of meat or vegetable will go a long way when it is chopped up and cooked again in the Chinese style. Leftovers are also good in Chinese soups and salads.

To keep food for a time in the refrigerator you need a supply of jars with lids and plastic containers. Never leave food sitting uncovered in the refrigerator. Not only does it absorb or create food odors but it will look so unappetizing the next day that no one will want to do anything with it.

You'll often find yourself using only half a can of bamboo shoots or bean sprouts—or any other vegetable for that matter. Save them in a jar and use them the next day in another dish. Learn to plan leftovers.

In this section you will find basic Chinese recipes for leftover food. You can change them and substitute other meats or vegetables in them as you please.

EGG FOO YUNG

This is the cliché of Chinese foods, but it is an excellent way to use up leftover vegetables. It is great served on its own at lunch or with another dish at dinner.

1 can (7 oz.) crab meat, drained
4 scallions
½ can (5 oz.) bamboo shoots, drained
½ can (5 oz.) bean sprouts, drained
2 dried Chinese mushrooms, soaked in water overnight (or for 30 min.)
½ c. peas (leftover, optional)

6 eggs
1 tsp. powdered ginger
1 tblsp. white wine
Salt and pepper
½ c. peanut or vegetable oil
1 c. chicken stock
2 tblsp. soy sauce
1 tblsp. cornstarch mixed with
1 tblsp. water

Mince crab meat. Chop scallions, bamboo shoots, bean sprouts, and drained mushrooms. Place in bowl with peas. In another bowl beat eggs. To them add ginger, wine, and crab meat. Mix together and season. In skillet heat half the oil. Fry the egg mixture into one large omelet or four small ones, made separately. Remove from pan. Add remaining oil. Add vegetables and stir-fry for 1 minute. Add stock, soy sauce, and cornstarch mixture. Bring to boil and cook until sauce coats spoon. Pour over omelets and serve. Serves 4.

LEFTOVER VEGETABLE OMELET

This is a good way to use up leftover vegetables. They must be heated separately and added to the omelet when it is nearly done.

1-1½ c. finely chopped leftover vegetables
2 tsp. soy sauce
Salt and pepper

6 eggs
2 tsp. peanut or vegetable oil

Chop vegetables as finely as possible. Add soy sauce and seasoning. Heat over very low heat in saucepan. Beat eggs and season. Heat omelet pan and oil. When hot add eggs; pull in sides with fork, and when almost done but still runny on top pour in the vegetables. Serves 4.

LEFTOVER BEEF CHOW MEIN
WITH LETTUCE HEARTS

You don't need to serve anything else with this dish, except perhaps a salad. Save the rest of the lettuce for the salad.

You can use celery or cabbage hearts for this recipe.

1 lb. cooked beef
1 lb. lettuce hearts
3 scallions
1 clove garlic
1 slice ginger
3 tblsp. peanut or vegetable oil

2 tblsp. soy sauce
1 tblsp. dry sherry
3 c. cold cooked noodles
Salt and pepper

Slice beef paper thin in 1 inch strips. Chop hearts and scallions. Crush garlic and chop ginger. In skillet heat oil. Stir-fry hearts and scallions for 2 minutes. Add garlic and ginger, stir-fry for 2 more minutes. Add beef and fry for 1 minute. Pour in soy sauce and sherry, stir. Add noodles and cook for 3 minutes until

beef and noodles are hot. Season and serve at once.
Serves 4.

LEFTOVER ROAST BEEF SALAD

Use rare roast beef and let it stand in the dressing
for half an hour before you serve it. Don't add the cucumber to the salad until the last minute. Slice it and
let stand in salt until you are ready to use it. This will
absorb the excess water.

1 lb. roast beef	4 scallion tops
4 tomatoes	1 cucumber
1 onion	

Dressing

1 tblsp. soy sauce	Salt and pepper
2 tblsp. peanut or vegeta- ble oil	1 tsp. sesame seeds (op- tional)

Shred the roast beef. Slice the tomatoes and onion.
Chop the scallion tops. Peel and slice the cucumber.
Let stand salted. Mix dressing and toss over other ingredients except cucumber. Let stand for half an
hour. Mix cucumber in salad and serve. Serves 4.

LEFTOVER CHICKEN WITH BEAN SPROUTS

Solving the problem of leftover chicken, instead of
the dull salad and cold chicken meals that tend to follow a roast, the Chinese have a hundred different
ways of cooking it again. And, of course, you don't
need very much since the Chinese use one-quarter of
the meat in a meal that we do. All you need to buy
here is a can of bean sprouts. We suggest rice and
perhaps a cucumber and tomato salad to go with it.

Remember that the chicken stock *must* be hot when you add it.

2 tblsp. peanut or vegetable oil
2 scallions, chopped
1 can (5 oz.) bean sprouts, drained
4 tblsp. long strips cooked chicken (or more if you have more to use up)
½ c. chicken stock (½ cube melted in ½ c. hot water or ½ c. bouillon)

2 tsp. dry sherry
1 tsp. soy sauce
½ tsp. cornstarch mixed with
1 tsp. water
Salt and pepper

Heat skillet and add oil. When hot add scallions and fry for 1 minute. Add bean sprouts and cook for 2 minutes. Season and transfer to side dish. Add chicken and cook over high heat for 1 minute. Add hot chicken stock and bring to boil. Add sherry and soy sauce. Stir in cornstarch mixture, cook for 1 minute more. Season and return bean sprouts and scallions to pan. Heat through, pour into dish. Serves 4.

LEFTOVER CHICKEN WITH PINEAPPLE

The chicken is added at the end and heated through. It should not cook or it will become dry and tasteless. You can use this recipe for fresh chicken if you wish, in which case add it to the pan after the vegetables.

Serve the meal with rice and a green vegetable.

½ can (5 oz.) bamboo shoots
½ can (5 oz.) water chestnuts
6 Chinese dried mushrooms, soaked in water overnight (or for 30 min.)
2 tsp. cornstarch mixed with
2 tsp. dry sherry
1 tsp. soy sauce
1 tsp. brown sugar
3 tblsp. peanut or vegetable oil
4 slices ginger, chopped (or 1 tsp. powdered)
½ c. chicken stock (or mushroom liquid)
¼ c. juice from pineapple chunks
½ 1-lb. can pineapple chunks, drained
2 c. cut-up chicken meat
Salt and pepper

Drain and slice the bamboo shoots, water chestnuts, and mushrooms. In bowl mix together cornstarch and sherry, soy sauce, and sugar. In skillet heat oil. Add ginger and stir-fry with vegetables for 3 minutes. Add stock, pineapple juice, and sherry-soy sauce mixture. Bring to boil. Turn down heat and add pineapple chunks and chicken. Season and cook for about 3 minutes so that the ingredients are heated and the sauce thickens to coat the spoon. Serves 4.

LEFTOVER CHINESE CHICKEN SALAD

You can serve this either as a luncheon or as a buffet dish. You can also invent additions (a hard-boiled egg sliced over it for example). The dish is very light so you may want to serve it with something else-cold meat, or perhaps another salad item—such as cold stuffed peppers.

4 large white mushrooms (or Chinese dried, soaked overnight) (or for 30 min.), drained
½ c. chicken stock
½ c. (5 oz.) bean sprouts, drained
3 tblsp. white wine vinegar
1 tsp. soy sauce
4 tblsp. oil
6 tblsp. cut into thin strips cold leftover chicken
½ lettuce, cut into thin strips
Salt and pepper

Cook mushrooms for 10 minutes, covered, in chicken stock. Remove and slice thinly. Add bean sprouts to stock. Cook for 3 minutes. Remove and drain. Mix dressing: vinegar, soy sauce, and oil in bowl. Add mushrooms, bean sprouts, chicken, and lettuce. Season and serve. Serves 4.

LEFTOVER CHICKEN WITH SWEET AND SOUR SAUCE*

This is one of the most delicious ways to serve chicken again. The meat is diced and heated in broth while the Sweet and Sour Sauce* is made in a separate pan. Decorate the dish with chopped scallion tops.
Serve this with rice and a Chinese vegetable.

2 c. diced cooked chicken meat	Sweet and Sour Sauce*
1 c. chicken stock	2 scallions, including tops chopped

Heat chicken in stock. Meanwhile make Sweet and Sour Sauce*. Remove chicken from stock and place on heated plate. Spoon sauce over, scatter with scallions, and serve. Serves 4.

SPINACH AND LEFTOVER HAM

The ham is heated in chicken broth just long enough for the spinach to cook without toughening the ham. This dish can be a complete one in itself if you drop in an egg for each person and let it poach in the stock with the other ingredients. The eggs must be absolutely fresh though or they will become stringy.

1 lb. spinach	Salt and pepper
4 thick slices ham	4 c. chicken stock
1 tblsp. soy sauce	4 eggs (optional)
1 tblsp. dry sherry	

Clean and chop the spinach. Cut the ham slices into strips about ½ inch by 2 inches. In pan put soy sauce, sherry, seasoning, and stock. Bring to boil, add ham and spinach (and optional eggs), and simmer for 4 minutes. Serve immediately. Serves 4.

FRIED BAMBOO SHOOTS WITH HAM

This is a very good way of using up roast ham. Serve it with sweet potatoes or rice, and a green vegetable.

You may substitute fresh pork or leftover pork for this dish with equally good results.

1 lb. ham, diced	1 can (5 oz.) bamboo
4 tblsp. soy sauce	shoots
1 tsp. dry sherry	8 tblsp. peanut or vegetable oil
2 tsp. brown sugar	
1 tsp. cornstarch mixed with	2 scallions, chopped
1 tsp. water	Salt and pepper

Dredge the ham with a marinade made of the soy sauce, sherry, sugar, and cornstarch mixture and reserve marinade. Drain bamboo shoots. In skillet heat oil. Stir-fry ham for 2 minutes. Add bamboo shoots and scallions. Stir-fry for 2 minutes. Add marinade mixture to pan. Bring to boil and when sauce thickens to coat spoon, season and serve. Serves 4.

LEFTOVER HAM WITH HARD-BOILED EGGS

One of the most difficult tasks after Easter is finishing up the ham. It becomes so monotonous after a while when it is served up again and again in the same way.

The sauce here is much like a Sweet and Sour Sauce*. You can add pineapple chunks to it at the end for a variation. Score the eggs before you add them to the pan so that the sauce penetrates easily.

1 lb. ham	½ c. soy sauce
1 onion	1 tsp. molasses
2 tblsp. peanut or vegetable oil	4 tblsp. dry sherry
	Salt and pepper
2 tsp. chopped dill	6 hard-boiled eggs

Slice the ham and the onion. In skillet heat oil. Fry dill and onion until onion is clear. Add ham and fry on both sides. Stir in soy sauce, molasses, and sherry, and seasoning, and simmer for 15 minutes, turning the ham once or twice. Add the eggs and simmer for 10 minutes more. Serves 4.

LEFTOVER LAMB CHOW MEIN WITH MUSHROOMS AND CELERY

If you use dried mushrooms don't forget to soak them overnight or for 30 minutes. You can use bamboo shoots or bean sprouts in this recipe if you have any half cans that you need to use up. You won't need anything else with this meal. If you want to have a salad, we suggest a cucumber or watercress salad.

1 lb. cooked lamb	1 slice ginger
½ lb. dried Chinese mushrooms soaked overnight (or for 30 min.), drained, or fresh	3 tblsp. peanut or vegetable oil
	2 tblsp. soy sauce
	1 tblsp. dry sherry
½ lb. celery	3 c. cold cooked noodles
3 scallions	Salt and pepper
1 clove garlic	

Chop lamb into 1 inch cubes. Slice mushrooms and celery. Chop scallions, crush garlic, and chop ginger. In skillet heat oil. Stir-fry garlic and ginger for 1 minute, add scallions and celery. Cook for 1 minute, add mushrooms. After 1 minute add lamb; brown and pour in soy sauce and sherry. Stir. Add noodles and cook for 3 minutes until lamb and noodles are hot. Season and serve at once. Serves 4.

LEFTOVER SWEET AND SOUR PORK WITH PINEAPPLE

Add the pork to the pan at the end so that it does not get overcooked and dry. You can use smoked bacon or fresh pork equally well here, but it should be added to the pan before the vegetables.

1 lb. pork meat	2 tblsp. chicken stock
2 green peppers	2 tblsp. vinegar
1 chili pepper	¼ c. juice from canned pineapple
1 tomato	
1 onion	1 tsp. cornstarch mixed with
4 tblsp. peanut or vegetable oil	
	2 tsp. water
1 tsp. tomato paste	½ 1-lb. can pineapple chunks, drained
1 tblsp. brown sugar	
1 tsp. salt	Pepper

Chop the pork meat into 1 inch pieces. Seed and chop the green peppers, chili pepper. Drop tomato into boiling water to remove skin. Chop. Chop onion. In skillet heat oil. Stir-fry vegetables for 3 minutes. Add tomato paste, sugar, salt, chicken stock, vinegar, and pineapple juice. Bring to boil. Add cornstarch mixture and stir until sauce is thick enough to coat spoon. Add pork and pineapple chunks; stir until heated through. Season and serve. Serves 4.

LEFTOVER TURKEY SALAD

To stretch this salad you can add half a cup of cold cooked rice with a teaspoonful of soy sauce. If you wish, squeeze some lemon juice over the avocado to stop it from turning brown.

2 c. chopped turkey meat	1 tblsp. soy sauce
1 avocado, peeled and pitted	2 tblsp. peanut or vegetable oil
1 can (5 oz.) bean sprouts	1 tsp. vinegar
3 scallion tops	½ tsp. paprika
1 tsp. Tabasco sauce	Salt and pepper

Slice avocado. Drain bean sprouts. Chop scallion tops. In a cup or bowl mix Tabasco sauce, soy sauce, oil, vinegar, paprika, and seasoning. Pour over meat, avocado slices, bean sprouts, and scallions; toss and serve. Serves 4.

Index

225

230

Variety Cookbooks

Dine like a king at home! Unbelievably priced for everyone's pocket. Easy to read and follow directions. Recipes for simple to gourmet taste buds.

- ☐ **Budget Cooking for Four**
  $2.00 Dinners For Four

- ☐ **The Buffet Cookbook**

- ☐ **Chinese Cooking with American Meals**

- ☐ **Cooking With Eggs**

- ☐ **The New Hamburger Cookbook**

- ☐ **The New Hotdog Cookbook**

- ☐ **The Practical Fondue Cookbook**

- ☐ **The Quick & Easy Cookbook**

- ☐ **Savory Stews**

- ☐ **The Seafood Cookbook**

MODERN PROMOTIONS/PUBLISHERS
155 East 55 Street, New York, N.Y. 10022

ONLY $1.75, plus $1.00 for postage and handling for each book.
(In Canada please add $1.50 P&H for each book.)

Name_____

Address_____

City_____ State_____ Zip_____

I enclose $_____ for_____ books which includes all postage and handling costs.
(No C.O.D.'s please)